THE NEW NATURALIST

BUMBLEBEES

by

JOHN B. FREE

M.A., PH.D.

and

COLIN G. BUTLER

M.A., PH.D., F.R.P.S.

Bee Department
Rothamsted Experimental Station

With two appendices by

IAN H. H. YARROW

M.A., PH.D.

Entomology Department
British Museum (Natural History)

Illustrated with 46 photographs
by Colin G. Butler

COLLINS
ST JAMES'S PLACE, LONDON

First published 1959
Reprinted 1968

To our wives—
in gratitude

Printed in Great Britain
Collins Clear-Type Press
London and Glasgow

Ye must perdonne my wyttes, for I tell you plaine,
I have a hive of humble bees swarmynge in my brain.

UNKNOWN. *Respublica*

CONTENTS

CONTENTS

LIST OF PLATES

LIST OF FIGURES

NAMES OF BUMBLEBEES SHOWN IN COLOUR FRONTISPIECE

Left column (reading from top to bottom): 1 *Bombus terrestris* QUEEN;
2 *Bombus terrestris* WORKER; 3 *Bombus lucorum* QUEEN;
4 *Bombus lucorum* WORKER; 5 *Bombus lucorum,* MALE; 6 *Bombus lapidarius* QUEEN
Centre column: 7 *Bombus lapidarius* MALE; 8 *Bombus pratorum* QUEEN; 9 *Bombus pratorum* WORKER; 10 *Bombus hortorum* WORKER; 11 *Bombus hortorum* MALE; 12 *Bombus hortorum* QUEEN
Right column: 13 *Bombus agrorum* QUEEN; 14 *Bombus agrorum* MALE;
15 *Psithyrus vestalis* QUEEN; 16 *Psithyrus vestalis* MALE;
17 *Psithyrus rupestris* MALE; 18 *Psithyrus rupestris* QUEEN

EDITORS' PREFACE

Dr. Colin Butler, Head of the Bee Department at Rothamsted Experimental Station, and one of the world's most distinguished hymenopterists, will already be familiar to readers of the New Naturalist Series as the author of *The World of the Honeybee*. This now classic monograph was remarkable for many things, not least for Dr. Butler's lucid exposition of his new and important theory of *queen substance*.

In this new book he is joined by his colleague, Dr. John B. Free. Like Butler, Free has been interested in animal behaviour—and in particular bee behaviour—ever since he was an undergraduate at Cambridge. Indeed, the careers of both have been very similar. Whilst at Cambridge, where he took Part II of the Natural Sciences tripos in Zoology, Free was encouraged to study bumblebees and their behaviour by Dr. W. H. Thorpe, F.R.S., perhaps the world's greatest authority on animal learning. So great did Free's interest become in this group of insects that in July 1951, after graduating, he was able to obtain a three-year grant from the Agricultural Research Council to continue his studies of bumblebee behaviour under his co-author at Rothamsted. For his work during this period he obtained the PH.D. degree of London University; and he subsequently joined the permanent staff of the Bee Department. Already he has published some twenty scientific papers on bees—mostly on bumblebees, but quite a number on honeybees—several of the latter in collaboration with Butler. Many of the experiments described in this remarkable new work were carried out by Free whilst he has been at Rothamsted.

The Editors of the *New Naturalist* are confident that this happy collaboration will widely encourage naturalists all over the world to take up the study of bumblebees. They are social insects whose communities are at a state of cohesion and organisation more primitive than that of honeybees, and therefore of deep interest from the evolutionary point of view.

The authors' enthusiasm for field research will prove infectious. Of great importance is their demonstration that wild bumblebees are easily kept under study conditions; they have included the most valuable appendices upon the finding of bumblebees' nests and upon their capture and maintenance. There can be no doubt that from this new addition to our series, which the Editors recommend most heartily, new advances in our understanding of insect behaviour will flow. Our readers will also find that this book has been illustrated by photographs as skilful and original as those which aroused such interest in Butler's *Honeybee* monograph. Furthermore, appendices are also included upon the identification and distribution of all the British species of bumblebee. These have been prepared by Dr. Ian H. H. Yarrow of the British Museum (Natural History). This most valuable contribution is the final touch which makes *Bumblebees* the definitive handbook to the British species, as well as an original and classic contribution to our knowledge of the instincts and habits of social insects.

THE EDITORS

AUTHORS' PREFACE

THE first monograph to deal exclusively with the British bumblebees, or humblebees as they are sometimes called, was *The
Humble-bee* by F. W. L. Sladen, which was published in 1912.
This fine work, which has been in much demand by naturalists
in general and by students of bumblebees in particular, has long
since been out of print and is now almost unobtainable. Since
Sladen's day considerable advances have been made in our
knowledge of bumblebees by workers in many countries; and in
preparing this treatise for The New Naturalist series we have
attempted to give a complete and up-to-date picture of the
behaviour and social life of the bumblebee. Much has still to
be learnt, however, and throughout this book we have indicated
some of the more obvious gaps in our knowledge.

Whilst trying to maintain continuity throughout the book we
have made each chapter as complete as possible in itself. The
detailed subject-index will, we trust, enable those interested in
particular aspects of the biology of bumblebees to experience
little difficulty in finding the relevant information. References
to much of the important literature have also been given, but at
the same time we have endeavoured not to interrupt the flow of
the text, whilst still providing sufficient references to enable the
reader to pursue his individual interests far beyond the scope of
this book.

Use of scientific terminology has been restricted to the minimum but it has been necessary to use the Linnean names of
different species of bumblebee if for no other reason than that no
adequate common English names exist. We have, furthermore,
often had occasion to refer to bumblebee species which are found
in countries other than our own in order to make the story
complete.

As it is most important to be able to identify the British

bumblebees correctly, we have asked Dr. I. H. H. Yarrow of the British Museum (Natural History), for whose cooperation we are most grateful, to prepare a key for the identification of the British species and to give an account of their distribution which we are glad to be able to include as appendices.

In the course of preparation of this book we have become aware of the great interest that people, ranging from schoolboys to professional biologists have for the bumblebee, and have received many queries on how to find their nests and keep them in captivity. We have accordingly included appendices giving information on these subjects, which we hope will be found useful.

We wish to take this opportunity of thanking Miss Marion Nunn for her secretarial assistance and Miss Inge Riedel for her help with some of the German literature. We are especially grateful to our wives for the many different ways in which they have helped us. Finally we are indebted to The *New Naturalist* Editors, especially to Sir Julian Huxley, F.R.S., for their invaluable help.

J. B. F.
C. G. B.

Harpenden

CHAPTER I

INTRODUCTION

Burly, dozing humble-bee,
   Where thou art is clime for me.
Let them sail for Porto Rique,
   Far-off heats through seas to seek;
I will follow thee alone,
   Thou animated torrid-zone!

Wiser far than human seer,
   Yellow-breeched philosopher!
Seeing only what is fair,
   Sipping only what is sweet,
Thou dost mock at fate and care,
   Leave the chaff, and take the wheat.

EMERSON. *The Humble-Bee*

THE bumblebees, are among our largest and most colourful insects, and there are some 25 different species of them in this country alone. Unlike the vast majority of insects, bumblebees are social in their behaviour and live together in colonies. Each colony is essentially a family consisting of the mother bumblebee, who is commonly called the queen, and her offspring (Pl. 11, p. 50). The majority of her daughters are sexually undeveloped, and are known as workers; it is usually only after several generations of workers have been reared that males and fully-developed females or queens, who are capable of founding colonies of their own, appear.

In the first few chapters of this book we will follow the life-history of a bumblebee colony from its initiation by an individual queen in the spring until it dies out in the summer or autumn. The young queens that have been reared in it will by this time have mated and left the parental nest to find sheltered places where they will remain until the following spring. The old mother queen and her workers all die long before winter sets in.

Our knowledge of bumblebees has gradually been pieced together during the last two centuries. The earlier writings contain many fanciful notions, and at the beginning of the 18th

century the queen was still regarded as a 'king' who was supposed
to direct the activities of his subjects. Anybody interested in the
earlier literature will find that the writings of Réaumur, Huber,
Lepeletier, Putnam, Hoffer and Wagner will repay study. The
results of their patient work, together with the notable contributions of F. W. L. Sladen, who lived in Kent at the beginning of
the present century, form the foundations of the early chapters
of this book.

The efficiency of any society is increased if the work that is
necessary to maintain it is divided amongst its individual
members, and insect societies are no exception to this general
rule. In a bumblebee colony there is an efficient division of
labour not only between the mother queen and her workers, but
also amongst the workers themselves, so that each individual
works for the good of her colony as a whole. We shall discuss how
this division of labour is organised and maintained, and how
adaptable it is to meet the changing needs of a colony.

The evolution of bees and flowers has gone hand in hand
and their relationship is a fascinating study on its own. Flowers
benefit from bee visits because the bees incidentally transfer pollen
from the male to the female organs and so bring about pollination
and enable seed to be produced. Competition for bees and other
insects as pollinating agents has undoubtedly played an important role in the evolution of flowering plants, since the colour,
shape and scent of their flowers all play a part in attracting such
visitors. The great services that bumblebees perform in the
pollination of agricultural and horticultural crops has probably
yet to be fully realised, although their value as pollinators of
various leguminous and fruit crops is well established. (See
Chapter 15, p. 130).

Bees have come to depend for their food on pollen and nectar
which, of course, they collect from flowers. Pollen provides the
protein in a bee's diet, whilst nectar, which consists almost

---

Plate *1* (*opposite*). QUEEN BUMBLEBEE, *Bombus agrorum*, FORAGING FOR HER
                    COLONY

In spring and early summer each overwintered queen attempts to found her
own colony for which she alone has to forage until her first worker offspring
appear. Note that the queen's wings have already become tattered and torn.
(x 2·5)

Plate 1

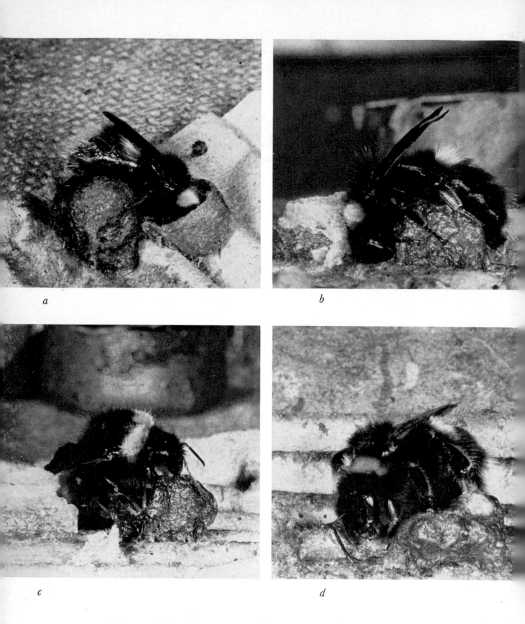

Plate 2.—Nest Founding by Captive Queens. *B. pratorum* (all x 1.9)

a. Queen clasping larval clump whilst feeding from honeypot.
b. Queen incubating larval clump.
c. Queen manipulating wax.
d. Queen with early larval clump.

entirely of a watery solution of various sugars, particularly of glucose, fructose and sucrose, provides the necessary carbohydrates. In common with other bees, the bumblebees are specialised in various ways for the collection of nectar and pollen. When visiting flowers a bumblebee often becomes dusted with their pollen which is effectively trapped in the long plumose hairs covering her body. With her fore-legs she brushes the pollen grains attached to the hairs of her head and the front part of her body forwards to her mouth-parts and moistens them with nectar, which causes them to stick together, and they are then passed back to the hindlegs. The outer, concave surface of the tibia of each hind-leg is highly polished and is surrounded by a fringe of long, curved hairs, thus forming the so-called 'pollen-basket' in which the pollen is carried back to the nest. (Pl. 18a, b, p. 99).

The mouth-parts of a bumblebee consist of a pair of biting jaws, or mandibles, which are used for various purposes, and a long proboscis or tongue which is used for sucking up nectar (Pl. 17, p. 98). When not in use the proboscis is not rolled up, but folded back beneath the head. Any liquid which a bumblebee ingests passes into its crop, or honey-stomach, where it can be temporarily stored. When the honey-stomach is empty, its walls are thrown into numerous folds, but when it is full all the folds disappear and the walls stretch until the honey-stomach resembles a miniature balloon. In it a bumblebee can carry nearly her own weight of nectar.

There can be few species of animals or plants which do not form the food of some other organism, and bumblebees are no exception to this rule. Not only do bumblebees often have a struggle to obtain enough food for themselves and their young, but they are also, both as individuals and as a colony, continually exposed to the attacks of other animals as diverse as shrews and nematode worms. But they defend themselves and their nests both by biting and stinging.

A bumblebee's sting consists of a long tapering shaft, which is connected with a poison-sac within her body. When a bee thrusts her sting into the body of her adversary, poison from this sac is injected down the canals in the shaft into its tissues. The sting of the bumblebee is derived from an egg-laying organ known as an ovipositor, which many insects, including near relatives of the bees, possess. The ovipositors of some insects have become adapted as piercing instruments for inserting their eggs into the tissues of plants, under bark, or into the ground, and even (in the case of many parasites) into the bodies of insects and other animals. In the bees this instrument is, however, no longer concerned with egg-laying and has become modified to serve as a weapon of offence and defence.

Mention must also be made of the wax-producing glands of the female bumblebee. These wax-glands are situated on both the upper and lower surfaces of the abdomen, and their ducts, from which thin 'scales' of wax emerge, open to the exterior between the segments. The bees take the wax scales from the surfaces of the glands with their hind-legs and mould them in their jaws when forming their combs.

Before we discuss the lives of bumblebees in detail let us consider their world distribution. In contrast to most social insects bumblebees occur much more abundantly in temperate than in tropical climates. They are distributed throughout Europe, Asia, North and South America, and in Africa north of the Sahara. Their northern limits extend above the 70th Parallel and thus well into the Arctic Circle, and they have been reported as far south as the tip of S. America. They are not indigenous to either Australia or New Zealand, but were successfully introduced into the latter country at the end of the last century.

In tropical countries bumblebees are on the wing the whole year round, but in temperate climates their colonies are annual affairs, the young mated queens alone surviving the winter and appearing in the spring, each to attempt to found a new colony. The further north one goes the later in the year do the first bumblebees appear, until at the northernmost limit of their range they are only flying during the few weeks of the brief sub-arctic summer.

CHAPTER 2

THE FOUNDING OF THE COLONY

But when was ever honey made
With one bee in a hive?

THOMAS HOOD. *The Last Man*

THE story of a bumblebee colony begins in spring with a single
bee, a queen, for the only bumblebees which manage to
survive throughout the winter in Britain and other temperate
parts of the world are young queens who were reared and mated
in the previous summer or autumn; they have not yet laid any
eggs. It is these overwintered, impregnated queens who form
the link between one generation and the next and who survive to
found new colonies, and so to perpetuate their species from year
to year.

In spring when the weather is becoming warmer and the
early flowers have opened, the first queen bumblebees appear,
having crawled from their winter quarters after seven or eight
months' rest. Queens of the different species appear at different
times in spring. One of the very earliest, which usually emerges
from hibernation in March, is *B. pratorum*, a small bee with a
reddish tip to her abdomen (Frontispiece, No. 8). Queens of many
other species often appear in April, whilst some, such as *B. lapidarius* (Frontispiece, Nos. 6, 7), are not seen in any numbers until
May or early June. Although we do not know for certain why the
queens of some species appear so much earlier than those of
others, it seems probable that the earlier ones do not require
such high environmental temperatures to arouse them from the
comatose state in which they have spent the winter.

At first the newly awakened queens are weak and drowsy,
and they often warm themselves in the sunshine for some time

before flying off. For the first few weeks the queens merely search the flowers to obtain food for themselves and eat a good deal of pollen as well as nectar. At night and in cold weather they take shelter, probably under debris or in the soil, and become quite torpid once more; but they come out again as soon as conditions become favourable. Some sites appear to be especially favoured as night quarters. For instance, Professor Bols of Belgium described in 1937 how when watching about ten square yards of a bank he saw no less than 30 *B. ruderatus* queens and 50 *P. rupestris* females creep down beneath a layer of old leaves which was covering it. Some of the queens very quickly pushed their way down under the leaf-mould and in about five minutes each was resting under a little mound about the size of a man's hand. As he had previously found queens hibernating in this same bank it seems possible that some of those he saw sheltering in the leaf-mould had previously hibernated in it and were returning to a place they already knew.

When the queens emerge from hibernation their ovaries are small and threadlike, but after they have been feeding themselves for a few weeks their ovaries begin to develop and the first eggs appear. At this stage in her development each queen, quite on her own, begins to search for a suitable place in which to make her home: it seems probable that physiological changes associated with her developing ovaries bring about this alteration in her behaviour.

It is while they are searching for places in which to build their nests that queen bumblebees are so conspicuous in spring, as they fly low along hedgerows, banks and rough ground, alighting every now and then to inspect a promising site more closely. It may perhaps take a queen several days, even weeks, to find a suitable site. In 1953 Cumber described a mortal combat between two *B. lucorum* queens who were looking for nest-sites in a wood, and this led him to make the interesting suggestion that queen bumblebees may exhibit territorial behaviour similar to that of birds.

All species of bumblebees often make their homes in the abandoned nests of field-mice, voles and shrews—nests which consist of accumulations of fine pieces of grass, moss, leaves and other material collected by the former occupant. It has been suggested, however, that when there is plenty of suitable material available a queen will sometimes construct a nest for herself instead of using the deserted nest of a small mammal. The actual places in which a bumblebee queen looks for a nest-site depends very much upon her species. Some species (e.g. *B. lapidarius* and *B. terrestris*) seem to favour sites which are approached by underground tunnels often several feet long, whilst others (e.g. *B. hortorum*) prefer sites with tunnels only a few inches in length. Then, again, the queens of other species (e.g. *B. agrorum, B. ruderarius,* and *B. muscorum*) usually select nesting places on the surface of the ground, often under tussocks of grass, or under moss. However, several species will nest both above and below ground, although most of them tend to do one or the other; and there are a few species (e.g. *B. pratorum* and *B. sylvarum*) which make use of such a variety of places that one is never certain where one will find them next. They make their homes in disused birds' nests, in bundles of hay or straw, in the thatch of cottages and barns, under the roots of decaying trees, and, surprisingly often, in the stuffing of old sofas and discarded mattresses, etc. One of us even found a nest in a pocket of an old, but, according to its owner, far from discarded, fur coat! The nests of all species of bumblebees are occasionally found in such habitats, and those of subterranean species which attract attention often occur under the floors of garden sheds or under concrete paths.

In 1945 Skovgaard published the results of an extensive survey, made during the years 1930-1934, of the nesting-places of bumblebees in Denmark. He found that uncultivated, infrequently disturbed land, such as commons and permanent grassland, contained far more nests per unit area than cultivated land. It appeared that earth banks were especially favoured, particularly by *B. hortorum*. Curiously, perhaps, those banks which faced south were the least popular. Skovgaard considered that of the different types of habitats which he studied mice mostly preferred the banks, and he suggested that deserted mouse nests built in banks are likely to remain drier and, therefore, more suitable for use by bumblebees than those built in many other places. Neglected, overgrown gardens were also favourite nesting areas, especially for colonies of *B. agrorum* and *B. pratorum*. Whereas some species seemed to have preferences for definite types of locality, others, e.g. *B. lapidarius* and *B. terrestris,* were fairly versatile in their choice.

When she has found a suitable nest the queen bumblebee pushes her way into the centre of it and there burrows out a roughly circular chamber about an inch in diameter, which is thus connected to the world outside by a narrow tunnel through which the queen can just squeeze. She then teases out the nesting material and lines her chamber with the very finest of it, and for the next day or so she spends most of the time in her new home where the warmth of her body begins to dry off the nesting material. Occasionally she leaves the nest to find food for herself and on these flights she comes to learn with increasing accuracy the features of the surrounding landscape and the position of her nest in relation to neighbouring objects (see Chapter 14, p. 124).

Whilst in her nest the queen begins to produce wax, which issues in the form of thin sheets from between the segments of her abdomen; and she uses it to build her first egg-cell in the shape of a shallow cup on the floor in the centre of the nest cavity. Up to this time the queen has been bringing back to her nest nectar only, which she deposits in the surrounding nest material. Once her egg-cell is ready, however, the queen again goes foraging, but this time not only for herself but also for her future family; and, for the first time, she brings home loads of pollen as well as of nectar (Pl. 1, p. 2). As soon as she arrives home with a load of pollen the queen goes up to her empty egg-cell and, turning round to face away from it, holds both her hind-legs together over it and thrusts the pollen out of her pollen-baskets with rapid movements of her middle pair of legs so that it falls into the cell. She then turns round and with her mandibles smooths the pollen down into the cell before leaving the nest to collect more.

All this time, the queen has been eating a great deal of pollen and, as a result of the protein it contains, her ovaries have developed considerably, so that by the time she has provisioned her egg-cell with sufficient pollen she is ready to lay her first batch of eggs in it. The number of eggs laid in this first cell varies not only with the different species of bumblebees but also, to some extent, from queen to queen within a species. Generally speaking, however, the number varies between 8 and 14 in this first cell and it is probable that it takes the queen more than one sitting' to lay them. The eggs are sausage-shaped, each about 3-4 mm. long and 1 mm. wide. Directly she has laid her eggs the queen covers over the top of the cell with wax and so leaves the eggs in a chamber which has a floor of pollen, and walls and roof of wax, the whole structure being roughly spherical and about a quarter of an inch, or slightly more, in diameter (Fig. 1a, p. 11).

Some writers believe that instead of the wax egg-cell being made first and pollen deposited in it afterwards, the pollen is collected by the queen, moulded into a ball, and attached directly to the nesting material, and that the wax cell is then built on top of it. Possibly the order of events differs with the different species, and more evidence is required before this point can be settled; however, the important fact, agreed upon by all observers, is that the eggs rest on a bed of pollen and are covered with a canopy of wax.

Once the eggs have been laid, or just before, the queen begins to build a wax honeypot just inside the entrance of the nest-cavity and, as soon as she has completed its base and the beginnings of its sides, she uses it to store some of the nectar she has collected in the field (Pl. 3, p. 18). It takes a queen a day or two to complete her honeypot: when it is finished it may be anything up to ¾ inch high and ½ inch in diameter, although its size varies somewhat according to the species of queen. In it the queen stores honey* which helps to tide her over periods of bad weather when she cannot leave home to collect fresh food. The queen constantly alters the mouth of her honeypot; when it only contains a little honey it is left wide open, but when it is full it is often very nearly closed.

When the tiny, pearly white, larvae hatch from the eggs they immediately start to feed on the bed of pollen on which they find themselves. The queen, their mother, now not only has to find food for herself but also for her offspring, and she supplements their diet with honey and pollen. This she does by making a

---

*Little seems to be known about the composition of the "honey" found in bumblebees' combs. Honeybees concentrate nectar and convert a high proportion of its sugars into simpler ones, the resulting material being known as honey. Bumblebee honey may also be very concentrated but to what extent its sugars have been similarly converted appears to be unknown.

breach in the wall of their cell with her mandibles; with rapid contractions of her abdomen, she then regurgitates the food from her honey-stomach into the cell before sealing it up once more. The queens of some species squirt into the larval cell a mixture of honey and pollen, whilst those of others regurgitate honey only into the cell and plaster the pollen onto the side of it so that the larvae have to take it directly for themselves (Pl. 10b, p. 35). A queen of one of the species which feed their young with a mixture of honey and pollen, stores the pollen pellets, like a string of beads, around the outside of her larval group. These feeding processes are described in greater detail in Chapter 3, p. 17.

The larvae are maggot-like, have no distinct organs of locomotion, no eyes, and little in the way of other sense-organs. Lack of such organs is doubtless associated with the fact that the larvae live in perpetual darkness and do not need to seek their food actively as do the immature stages of many other insects.

The larvae grow very quickly during the ensuing days and change their skins several times. Every now and again, the queen incorporates more wax, which she has secreted, into the walls of their cell so that they still remain fully covered as they grow larger. When the larvae are full-grown their individual positions are easily recognised as bulges in the wall of their wax covering (Pl. 10b, p. 35). Feeding now ceases and the larvae prepare themselves for their transformation into pupae, each individual spinning a silken cocoon round itself and so becoming entirely separated from the other larvae in its cell. (Fig. 1b, c, p. 11).

Until this stage in their life-history has been reached none of

---

FIG. 1 (*opposite*) Cross sections of combs showing initial stages of Colony Founding (after Sladen 1912).
a. The nest cavity. The honeypot is near the nest entrance. The eggs are contained in a wax chamber and rest on a lump of pollen (stippled).
b. The eggs have hatched into larvae.
c. The larvae have spun their cocoons and changed into pupae (in the inside cocoons) and prepupae (in the outside cocoons). A second batch of eggs has been laid on top of the right hand cocoon.
d. Adult bees have emerged from the central cocoons of the first brood batch. The vacated cocoons are used for storing honey and pollen.
e. The comb grows upwards and outwards as new batches of brood are produced.

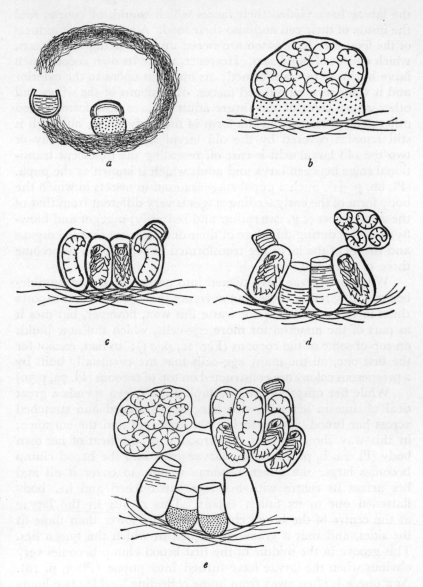

FIG I

the larvae have voided their faeces which would, of course, foul the inside of their cell and also their food. All the waste products of the food they have eaten are stored up in their digestive tracts, which consist of blind sacs. However, inside its own cocoon each larva begins to be transformed; its hind-gut opens to the exterior and it voids its accumulated faeces. Rudiments of the wings and other appendages of the future adult bee are now formed, and other general changes in the form of the body occur, although it still remains covered by the old larval skin. Within a day or two the old larval skin is cast off revealing the quiescent transitional stage between larva and adult which is known as the pupa. (Pl. 8b, p. 31). Such a pupal stage is found in insects in which the body form of the early feeding stages is very different from that of the adult insect (e.g. caterpillar and butterfly; maggot and blowfly) and it is during this stage of their development that the organs and tissues of the larva are transformed or remodelled to become those of the adult.

When her larvae have turned into pupae the queen bumblebee carefully removes the wax covering their cocoons and exposes them to view. She does not waste this wax, however, but uses it as part of the material for more egg-cells, which she now builds on top of some of the cocoons (Fig. 1c, p. 11); in fact, except for the first one, all the many egg-cells that are eventually built by a prosperous colony are constructed on top of cocoons (Pl. 7a, p.30)

While her offspring are developing the queen spends a great deal of time in her nest with her body flattened and stretched across her brood clump, facing her honeypot and the entrance; in this way she incubates the brood with the heat of her own body (Pl. 2a, b, p. 5). As the larvae grow and the brood clump becomes larger the queen becomes unable to cover it all and lies across its centre with her legs outstretched and her body flattened out to its fullest extent. This results in the larvae at the centre of the brood clump becoming lower than those at the sides, and thus a groove is formed in which the queen lies. This groove in the middle of the first brood clump becomes very obvious when the larvae have turned into pupae (Pl. 3, p. 18). As a queen is often away from home collecting food for two hours or more at a time it is clear, however, that the brood is able to survive for some time without incubation. At the end of the pupal stage the fully developed adult bees make their appearance, and the effect of the warmth of the incubating queen's body is demonstrated by the order in which they emerge. Those in the centre of the groove always emerge first, followed as a rule by those on either side of the groove, and lastly those right on the outside appear (Fig. 1d, p. 11).

No mention has yet been made of the duration of the developmental stages through which a bumblebee passes. Different observers have noted quite considerable differences in the lengths of the various stages; these may perhaps partly be accounted for by species differences, and partly by variations in the temperature at which the bees were reared, and also by the food-supply which was available to them (see Valle, 1955). To give but one example Brian (1951a) found that for *B. agrorum* the egg stage lasted from four to six days, the larval stage from ten to nineteen days and the pupal stage from ten to eighteen days. There was great variability in the rates at which the larvae in the different brood-batches developed; on several occasions she found that the adults produced from one batch of eggs actually emerged in advance of those from another batch of eggs laid some time before. This occurred in spite of the fact that variability in the times of emergence of the different adults reared from any one batch of eggs was usually no more than could be attributed to differences in the times at which the individual eggs were laid.

When she is ready to emerge from her cocoon the young bee gnaws her way through the top of it, often being helped to do so by her mother, and, pushing back the circular flap thus cut, she crawls out into the nest. At first she is very weak and unsteady on her legs; her coat is like silvery down and her wings lie limply along her back. During the next day or so she steadily gains strength; her coat dries out and takes on the colour-pattern typical of her species, and her wings harden and become functional. The young worker bee—for the first bees to be reared by a queen are all workers—is now fully prepared to undertake the eventful life that lies ahead, and the wonderful transformation from egg to perfect insect is complete.

Thus the colony, consisting of the queen and her first workers, is now a reality.

CHAPTER 3

THE GROWTH OF THE COLONY

The prescient female rears her tender brood
In strict proportion to the hoarded food.

EVANS

ONCE the first workers have emerged in a nest they very soon begin to carry out tasks which were formerly performed by the queen alone, so that a truly social unit in which a few workers and their mother cooperate to the common good comes into being. At first the queen has to forage to obtain food for her young workers, her brood and herself, but within a few days some of the workers start foraging regularly and thereafter the queen ceases to leave the nest and becomes exclusively occupied with indoor duties. The recent weeks of hard work have left their mark on her, however, and her coat is often badly worn in parts and her wing-tips frayed. It is obviously to the advantage of the colony that its most important individual—the mother of its future members—shall remain in the comparative safety of the nest rather than risk her life in the hazardous occupation of foraging. A queen bumblebee does not, however, simply become an egg-laying machine in the way that a queen honeybee does, but continues to help her workers to feed and incubate the brood and engages in other household tasks throughout her life.

We have seen that whilst her first batch of young are still pupae the queen builds more egg-cells on top of some of their cocoons (p. 12). These egg-cells are built slightly on the outer sides of the cocoons and so do not get in the way of the young bees as they are emerging. When a queen is ready to lay some eggs she inserts the tip of her abdomen into a cell and grips its sides and the surrounding part of the cocoon with her legs. The actual laying of the eggs is accompanied by twitchings of her legs and contractions of her abdomen, and her sting is extended out of the way of the eggs as they emerge from her abdomen and either rests on the brim of the egg-cell or is thrust through the side of it.

Soon after the queen's second batch of eggs has hatched the workers produced from the first batch are ready to help their mother to look after the new larvae. When in their turn these larvae pupate still more egg-cells are built on top of their cocoons, with the result that the comb expands in a somewhat irregular way both upwards and outwards (Fig. 1e, p. 11). These later batches of cocoons differ from the first in that there is no fixed brooding position and no brooding-groove is formed on them, and, indeed, the cells in the middle of a batch are actually higher than those at the sides (Pl. 10, p. 35).

As her colony grows in size, so the rate at which the queen bumblebee lays eggs increases, until, after a time, she may be laying a fresh batch of eggs every day. Cumber (1949a) dissected many queens and found that whilst their colonies are in the early stages of development some of the ripe eggs in the queens' ovaries are never laid but are reabsorbed instead. In this way things are arranged so that at any given time the queen does not produce more brood than can be properly looked after, under normal conditions, by the number of workers who are available. How this remarkable system of family limitation—for that is what it is —is brought about has recently been revealed by day-to-day observations made on the development of the brood in two colonies of *B. agrorum* by Brian (1951a). She found that the queens always constructed the egg-cells themselves—they did not leave the workers to do it—and that they built most of them on cocoons containing pupae that were not more than three days old. The number of eggs which each queen laid in a cell varied between four and sixteen, and all of them were laid within the period of a day or two. Now, in 1928 Frison published the results of some studies he had made on the development of an American species of bumblebee, *B. bimaculatus,* and was able to show that the average number of eggs laid by a queen in each cell tended to increase as her colony grew in size, and Brian, in her work, found that the actual number of eggs that a queen laid in any cell was proportional to the number of cocoons in the batch on top of which it was built. This means, of course, that as the batches come to contain more cocoons so the number of eggs laid in cells built on them also increases. Thus the number of eggs laid is adjusted to suit the number of workers that are going to be present to care for the larvae which will hatch from them, and in this way the balance between the number of workers and the amount of developing brood is maintained. It must not be thought, however, that all the eggs that are laid actually develop into adults. Indeed, Brian found that in the *B. agrorum* colonies which she studied, only about 30-40 per cent of them did so, and that mortality was greatest in the late egg and early larval stages. She suggested that this loss of potential workers may have been due to cannibalism, some of the larvae eating eggs and other young larvae. This is a suggestion which it would be interesting to investigate.

Unlike honeybees, bumblebees do not use the places vacated by newly emerged worker bees in which to rear further larvae. When the first workers of a bumblebee colony have emerged their empty cocoons are used to store food in (Fig. 1d, p. 11) and the old original honeypot built by the queen when she founded the colony falls into disuse and disrepair. When a worker bee bites her way out of her cocoon she leaves it with jagged edges; these the worker bees trim off neatly with their mandibles, and the height and capacity of the cocoons are also often increased by the building up of their walls with more wax. As a comb grows in size some of the older cocoons are no longer used as storage vessels and may become crushed and broken down; but in large nests of some species (e.g. *B. lucorum* and *B. terrestris*) the older cocoons at the bottom of the comb are often found to be full of thick honey and completely sealed over with wax. Cells constructed entirely of wax are found in some nests, and are usually situated on the periphery of the comb. Since they often only contain thin honey it seems probable that their contents are for immediate consumption, whilst the thick honey stored in the sealed cocoons serves as a reserve for use during unfavourable weather conditions when adequate fresh supplies cannot be obtained.

Some kinds of bumblebees also store their pollen in empty cocoons, which may be extended until they form tall wax cylinders as much as three inches high (e.g. *B. lucorum* and *B. terrestris,* Pl. 9a, p. 34). These storage cylinders for pollen mostly occur near the centre of the comb. Other species, however, (e.g. *B. agrorum* and *B. hortorum*) place the pollen they have collected into special wax pouches or pockets which they build on to the outside of the groups of larvae (Pl. 10b, p. 35). This difference in the way in which these two groups of bumble-bees store their pollen led Sladen in 1896 to classify them as "pollen-storers" and "pouch-makers" respectively; later he substituted the term "pocket-maker" for "pouch-maker". As we shall see, this classification of Sladen's is a very important one. The larvae of a pocket-making species feed directly on the pollen which is plastered into the pockets adjoining them: as the larvae grow the whole group expands in size and comes to have a mass of pollen both beside and underneath it. In addition the larvae of such a group may also perhaps feed on pollen that is regurgitated into their cells from time to time by the workers. The larvae of the pollen-storing species, on the other hand, are fed entirely on pollen and nectar regurgitated to them by the workers—apart, of course, from any pollen which may initially form the floor of their egg-cell.

As we have seen (Chapter 2, p. 9) a queen bumblebee, whatever her species, lays her first batch of eggs on top of a bed of pollen. Of some species those egg-cells which are built subsequently are also primed with pollen: as Sladen pointed out, it is noticeable that those species which prime all their egg-cells in this way belong to the pocket-making group, although it has since been found that this habit is also shared by an American pollen-storing species, *B. impatiens* (Plath, 1934), and by one of our own British pollen-storing species, *B. pratorum.*

It may well be asked how we know that the only kinds of food that bumblebee larvae receive are honey and pollen. After all, it is known that adult worker honeybees feed their larvae, in part, with a special food called "brood-food" which is very rich in protein; and that this brood-food is produced by a pair of glands—the pharyngeal glands—which worker and queen bumblebees also possess. How, then can we be sure that bumblebees do not feed their larvae on brood-food too? It is known that the workers in a honeybee colony who are actively engaged in feeding the larvae have large, turgid, pharyngeal glands, whereas those of other workers who are busy foraging and are not feeding the brood are quite small; and Free has been able to show that there is little or no difference in the size of the pharyngeal glands of the worker bumblebees who are busily engaged as foragers and those who stay at home and carry out nursing duties. Furthermore, he has shown that the pharyngeal glands of queen bumblebees appear to be just as fully developed when they emerge from their cocoons during the summer as they are when they are feeding their first larvae six or seven months later. Again, worker honeybees need to eat large quantities of pollen to obtain the protein that they must have before their pharyngeal glands can develop and secrete brood-food. If, therefore, the pharyngeal glands of bumblebees who are busily occupied with nursing duties were secreting brood-food, one would expect such bees to eat plenty of pollen, certainly much more than foragers do. However, dissection of large numbers of workers of both pollen-storing and pocket-making species has failed to show that the household bees eat any more pollen than the field bees. Further evidence against the idea that bumblebees produce and feed their larvae on brood-food, as honeybees do, has been provided by Bailey (1954) who studied the way in which the digestive tracts of both honeybees and bumblebees work. He came to the conclusion that bumblebees can only digest relatively small quantities of pollen in comparison with honeybees, and it therefore appears unlikely that they can obtain sufficient protein to enable them to secrete much in the way of brood-food. We must remember, however, that even though it seems improbable that bumblebees provide their larvae with this special kind of food, the possibility is not precluded that their pharyngeal and other glands may secrete digestive enzymes which become mixed with the food they regurgitate to their larvae, and so help in its digestion.

Plate 3 (*opposite*). AN EARLY STAGE IN COLONY DEVELOPMENT
An incubating queen normally faces her honey pot and nest entrance.
above. B. terrestris. Note well-defined groove of pupal clump in which queen lies while incubating. Honeypot is on right hand side. (x 2·0)
below. B. agrorum. Group of cocoons. (x 2·1)

Plate 4

All the larvae of the pocket-making species which are produced from the eggs laid in a single cell, feed on the same bed of pollen. This tends to keep them all together in a compact group, so that successive batches of brood are easily distinguishable from one another and the whole comb has an orderly appearance (Pl. 10, p. 35). On the other hand, the individual larvae of some of the pollen-storers, e.g. *B. lucorum*, *B. latreillellus* and *B. terrestris*, soon tend to become separated and each to become contained in its own separate compartment, so that it is much more difficult to decide which larvae have come from any single batch of eggs.

As a general rule bumblebee larvae are kept completely enclosed by wax, but in the case of some species, including the three just mentioned, small openings are left in the tops of the larval cells, a condition approaching that found in honeybees in which the cells remain open until shortly before the larvae are ready to pupate. So far as an adult bumblebee is concerned a larva appears to be something to be cared for only so long as it is enclosed in a wax covering; if the wax over a larva becomes slightly broken or torn the workers quickly repair it, but if the rent is a large one and a good deal of the larva is exposed then it is probable that the workers will throw it out of the nest. Larvae which workers find outside their cells are always treated in this way.

When one looks at a colony of bumblebees one of the things that strikes one most is that the workers vary a great deal in size. This is particularly noticeable in the case of the pocket-making species. This difference in the size of sister workers of the same colony is apparently a consequence of the smaller workers having received less food than the larger ones during larval life. When the larvae of the pocket-making species

---

Plate 4 (*opposite*). EXTERNAL VIEWS OF BUMBLEBEES' NESTS
Bumblebee queens frequently make use of the abandoned nests of mice in which to found their colonies.
above. *B. agrorum* nest showing entrance in centre. This species normally nests on the surface of the ground (x 1·0)
below. *B. lucorum* nest. This is an underground nesting species which sometimes builds a 'pseudo-nest', as shown, at the entrance to its burrow (x 1·3)

are about 5 days old, before the period in their lives when they grow most rapidly, each spins a flimsy silken partition between herself and her sister larvae, so that their positions relative to one another in the larval group become fixed. As Buttel-Reepen (1903), Sladen (1912) and Cumber (1949a) have pointed out, some of the larvae in such a group are better placed to obtain food than the others, and as a result grow much more quickly. In so doing they tend to push their less fortunate sisters further from the bed of pollen, further from the food, so that when the time comes for them to pupate some will have grown much larger than the others, a fact which is reflected in the sizes of the resulting adults. Those that were badly undernourished as larvae are often tiny and sometimes hardly recognisable as bumblebees at first sight; they may also have crippled wings.

Cumber has shown that the variation in size of the adults produced from a single batch of brood is less in the case of pollen-storers than it is in the case of pocket-makers. Such variations as still do exist among the pollen-storers can probably also be attributed to differences in the amounts of food obtained by different larvae.

The workers produced from the first eggs laid by a queen are often very small, sometimes no bigger than houseflies. It used to be thought that this was because the queen had to collect all the necessary food and rear them entirely on her own and that, in consequence, they had not been well nourished in their early stages. Indeed, Sladen (1912), Frison (1928) and Plath (1934) were led to believe that the average size of the bumblebees produced in a nest increases as the season progresses and food becomes more abundant. However, it was not until 1946, when Richards published his observations, that the first useful data on seasonal variation in the size of worker bumblebees were made available. Richards measured the size of the workers in three colonies of *B. agrorum* and classified each worker as "old", "moderately old", or "fresh" according to the condition (state of wear and tear) of her coat. He found that in each nest the "fresh" (i.e. younger) workers were on the average the largest,* thus quite definitely indicating a progressive increase in the sizes of the workers produced as these colonies had developed.

*Methods of measuring the size of worker bumblebees are given on page 161.

A few years later (Cumber 1949a) studied the same problem and came to a quite different conclusion. He collected a large number of colonies in various stages of development, and measured the sizes of the workers in each. From these measurements he concluded that in the case of the pocket-making bumblebee *B. agrorum* there is no gradual increase in the average size of the workers as their colonies develop as had previously been supposed, although he thought that there might be a tendency for some of those workers produced later in the season to be larger than those produced earlier.

How then can we account for the apparently conflicting results obtained by Richards on the one hand and by Cumber on the other? It might perhaps be argued that the condition of a worker's coat may not give a true indication of her age; but it can also be argued that the method which Cumber used to estimate any seasonal variations in the size of workers, is also subject to possible errors. Now, it is known from the work of Brian (1952) that those members of a bumblebee colony who are occupied with household duties and seldom leave the nest, tend to live longer than those who are engaged in the more wearing and hazardous occupation of foraging for food; and, since the latter tend to be the larger individuals (see p. 45), it follows that the average size of the workers found inside a nest when it is collected will tend to be smaller than that of all the workers who have been produced in it. The relatively greater proportion of small to large bees which, as Cumber found, are present in nests late in the season, is likely to offset any size increase resulting from the production of larger individuals, and the average size will tend to remain constant. Again, it must be remembered that it is seldom possible to catch all the bees when collecting a colony, and many of those who escape are undoubtedly foragers whom, as we have seen, tend to be the larger bees.

Brian (1951a) used a third method to determine the size of the workers produced at different stages of a colony's development. She measured the size of all the workers reared by two *B. agrorum* colonies throughout a season, but, unfortunately, neither of the two colonies produced many bees. Although she found that there was no regular increase in the size of the workers produced from successive brood batches, it appeared that unfavourable weather conditions probably influenced the size of the workers that emerged by affecting the amount of food the foragers were able to collect and, consequently, the amount of food supplied to the larvae.

We still do not know, therefore, whether the average size of the workers produced in a bumblebee colony generally does, or does not, increase as the season progresses. There seem to be two ways in which this information may be obtained. First one can adopt a method similar to that used by Cumber, but measure the size of the pupae present, rather than that of the adult workers. In fact Cumber did measure the pupae in some of his nests but, unfortunately, he did not obtain sufficient data to enable a sound conclusion to be drawn. Any such measurements would, of course, have to be made in several different years in order to try to eliminate any effects caused by weather conditions. The second method which can be used will involve keeping a colony in confinement, in a favourable and constant environment, throughout its life and measuring the weights of all the adult workers, or pupae, produced in it.

It has been mentioned earlier that queen bumblebees establish their colonies in a great variety of places and surround their combs with many different materials (Chapter 2, p. 7). As a colony grows in size and its comb becomes larger the original nesting material often becomes inadequate to cover it properly, and in the case of some species the workers add more material to it. The surface-nesting bumblebees, e.g. *B. agrorum* and *B. ruderatus*, the so-called carder bees, are particularly notable for this habit. The way in which bees of these species add to their nesting material is fascinating to watch. Each bee stands facing away from her nest and scrabbles any suitable material, such as pieces of grass or moss, that she can reach, backwards towards the nest-pile. In this way it is surprising how much and how quickly new material is added to the nest and carefully woven into place by the carder bees (Pl. 4a, p. 19). As a rule several well-defined passageways are made through this material so that

---

Plate 5 (opposite). A COLONY OF *Bombus lucorum*
One of the most prolific pollen-storing species. General view of exposed comb (x 1·2)

Plate 5

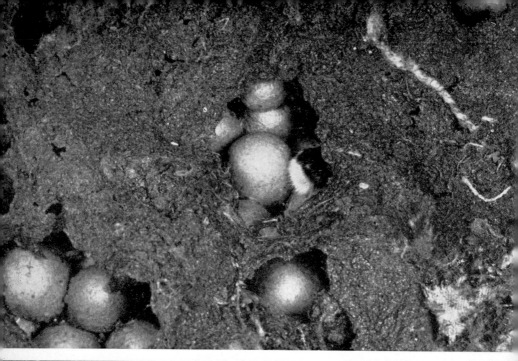

Plate 6

the foragers can quickly reach the comb when they arrive home.

Other kinds of bumblebees, who nest underground at the ends of tunnels, seem to have to make do with whatever nesting materials happen to be present when their colonies are started, but it is by no means unusual to find that the workers of such subterranean colonies have built small 'pseudo-nests', composed of grass, moss, etc., around the external openings of the entrance tunnels (Pl. 4b, p. 19).

The size which the comb of a colony attains varies very much in the different species, and also within a species. For instance, the combs of small colonies may never become more than 3-4 inches in diameter, whilst those of larger ones may be as much as 8-9 inches wide. The comb of a colony nesting on the surface of the ground is nearly always roughly circular in shape, whereas the combs of colonies which nest underground often have to be adapted to suit the shape of the nesting cavity and may even extend a little way along their entrance tunnels. Although early writers seem to have believed that bumblebees enlarge the size of their nest-cavities by removing particles of soil, no enlargement does in fact ever appear to take place. However, the old, empty cocoons at the bottom of a comb are often torn down and so more room is provided for the expanding brood. Fragments of such broken cocoons are sometimes to be found woven into the nesting material.

When prosperous, many colonies build canopies of wax over their combs. These canopies are attached to the sides of the combs, and supported over them by pillars at various points, and often have nesting material both worked into and covering them. Sufficient space is always left between the canopy and the top of the comb for the bees to move around freely (Pl. 6, p. 23). Some colonies almost entirely cover their combs with canopies,

---

Plate 6 (opposite). COMB PROTECTION BY *Bombus lucorum*
Some species of bumblebees, particularly those which dwell underground, often protect their combs with wax canopies.
above. The canopy is often incomplete. Any suitable materials available
become incorporated in it (x 2·0)
below. The canopy has been partly removed and the bees are busy repairing
the damage (x 1·8)

leaving just a few openings for the bees to pass in and out, but in other cases the canopies are no more than small discs over the centres of the combs.

If a strong colony is kept well fed a canopy covering the whole comb may appear in a day or two. Canopies are much more commonly built by those species which habitually nest underground than by those which nest above ground, and it seems likely that this habit may have been evolved to compensate for the smaller amount of nesting material usually available to underground colonies.

Wax is produced by worker bumblebees as well as by queens, and, as we have seen (Chapter 2, p. 8, 9), it is used for building egg-cells and honeypots and for enclosing the larvae, as well as for canopies. As a colony grows, more wax is continually being produced by the workers from the wax-glands on their bodies, and this, along with existing wax, is always being transferred to those places where it is most needed at the moment. For example, when the wax is removed from the cocoons of pupating larvae it is often used to build more egg-cells and honeypots, for building up the canopy, or to enlarge the coverings of larval groups.

It is obvious that both the nesting materials and the wax canopy which surround a comb must help to protect it from extremes of heat and cold. The efficiency of this form of insulation, combined with the temperature-regulating activities of the worker bees, has been measured by several people. Himmer (1933) showed that the body temperature of an individual bumblebee is on the average about 10°C. (50°F.) above that of the surrounding air and may rise to 16°C. (61°F.) above it; he found that the temperature inside a nest of *B. agrorum* remained at about 30°C. (86°F.). Cumber (1949a), working with colonies which had made their homes both above and below ground, found that even in the early stages of their development, when only a few workers were present, nest temperatures were always several degrees higher than that of the surrounding air and tended to fluctuate between 20-25°C. (68-77°F.). The larger the colony the higher and more constant its nest temperature remained.

Free measured the temperatures of colonies kept in nest-boxes, and found that the differences in temperature between the nest and the air outside became greatest at the beginning and end of each day. It therefore seems probable that the high proportion of the populations which were in the nests at these times helped to maintain the nest temperatures considerably above that of the outside air, and that when many of the bees were away foraging in the middle of the day, nest and outside temperatures tended to converge. We shall see later (p. 57) that even very few bees when placed together are able to raise the temperature of their surroundings to a considerable extent.

Bumblebees cannot only raise the temperatures of their nests above that of the outside atmosphere, but can also prevent them from becoming too hot. This they do by fanning currents of air over the surfaces of the combs with their wings. If one exposes a comb to the heat of the sun several workers soon climb on top of it and begin to cool it in this way. Nobody, however, seems to have tried to find out the temperature at which the bees first begin to cool their nests, nor to study the efficiency of the process. So far as we know bumblebees, unlike honeybees, never make use of the cooling effect of evaporating water to lower the temperatures of their homes.

CHAPTER 4

THE MATURITY AND DECLINE
OF THE COLONY

There's a whisper down the field where the year has shot her yield,
  And the ricks stand grey to the sun,
Singing: 'Once then, come over, for the bee has quit the clover,
  And your English summer's done.'

KIPLING. *The Long Trail*

THE number of workers produced can vary tremendously between one bumblebee colony and another. A thriving colony of one of our more prolific species, such as *B. lapidarius, B. lucorum,* or *B. terrestris,* will often rear as many as 300-400 workers during the season, whereas colonies of other species rarely produce more than 100. The largest colony that has so far been recorded was one of *B. medius,* which was found by Michener and Laberge (1954) in a tropical forest area of Mexico and which had produced no less than 2,183 worker bees. Of course variations in the number of bees produced occur not only between colonies of different species but also between colonies belonging to the same species and in the same year, and we may suppose that in these latter cases this is due in part to variations in the fertility of the queens heading the colonies concerned and partly to local conditions.

The production of males and virgin queens is always associated with the maturity or 'climax' of the bumblebee colony. At this stage in its development the temperature of the colony reaches its peak and fluctuates least, a condition which is no doubt of importance when these sexual forms are being reared. It must be pointed out, however, that many colonies succumb to the attacks of parasites (Chapter 10, p. 81), or die out during unfavourable weather conditions, before they reach this stage. Others never become sufficiently prosperous to produce any queens, but may succeed in rearing a few males. Still others produce queens but no males. When males and queens are reared, their numbers have been reported to vary from very few in the case of the smaller colonies to as many as 500 in the larger ones, as many or more than the number of workers available to rear them. These points are well illustrated by the fate of 80 colonies of *B. agrorum* which Cumber (1953) studied. He found that 48 of them failed to produce any sexual forms at all; 9 produced males only; 10 produced less than 8 queens each, and only 13 produced more than this number of queens.

Male bumblebees are produced from unfertilised eggs, and the cocoons in which the future males are contained cannot be distinguished from those which contain workers; but cocoons containing queens can often be recognised, as they tend to be larger than those of the other two castes.

In the case of those colonies that produce both males and queens, the males are usually produced first. For example, in *B. agrorum* colonies males are often initially produced in the same brood-clumps as workers; later on brood-clumps may appear which contain both males and queens, and finally pure queen brood only is produced.

The males of such species as *B. lucorum* and *B. pratorum* can readily be distinguished from the workers and queens by differences in the colouration of their coats, but in the case of other species the colouration of all three castes is identical (Frontispiece). There are, however, three ways in which the males can readily be distinguished from the females. First of all, unlike the workers and queens, the males do not possess stings; instead, a certain curiously shaped copulatory apparatus (genital armature) is clearly visible at the tip of their abdomens. Secondly, a male has 13 overlapping cuticular plates (tergites) covering the dorsal surface of his abdomen, whereas a worker or a queen only possesses 12. Thirdly, the antennae or feelers of a male are proportionately longer than those of a female (queen or worker) of the same species.

Both queen and worker bumblebees are produced from similar, fertilised eggs, and it is sometimes difficult to distinguish these two kinds of females from one another. Apart from the queens being usually somewhat larger and more bulky than workers of the same species, there are usually no colour or other external differences to be seen. The difference in size between queens and workers is most clearly marked in some of the pollen-storing species, such as *B. lapidarius, B. lucorum* and *B. terrestris.* Thus Cumber (1949a) found that the weights of workers of *B. lucorum* colonies ranged between 40–320 milligrams, whilst those of the queens varied from 460–700 milligrams. However, in other species, such as *B. pratorum* a pollen-storer, and *B. hortorum* a pocket-maker, such size-differences are not so well marked; whilst in some pocket-making species (e.g. *B. agrorum*) there are no distinct differences in size between the two castes, and it is sometimes difficult to tell whether a particular bee is a large worker or a small queen. In fact the only real difference between large workers and small queens is a physiological one. Cumber found that if he liberally fed both workers and queens the weights of the workers remained almost constant whereas those of the queens increased. When he subsequently dissected these bees he found that large, white, fat-bodies (food-storage organs) had been developed by the queens, but that the fat-bodies of the workers had remained undeveloped. Well-developed fat-bodies are, of course, necessary to queens who have to live upon their contents throughout the winter, but are unnecessary for the workers who die before the winter arrives. It is a remarkable fact that lavish feeding of young queens in autumn does not cause their ovaries to develop; instead they remain as thin threads until the following spring.

There has been a good deal of speculation, and some investigation, concerning the factors that cause a colony to give up rearing workers in favour of rearing queens. As long ago as 1922 Wheeler put forward a theory in an attempt to explain the production of the queen and worker castes in colonies of all social bees (honeybees, 'stingless' bees, and bumblebees). He supposed that those larvae which give rise to worker bees are inadequately nourished and, as a result, develop into small individuals, workers, with poorly developed ovaries. This would occur, particularly at the beginning of the season, when food is scarce and colonies have few foragers to collect it. He postulated that the strenuous life of nursing the larvae and foraging tends to keep the ovaries of worker bees from developing. He further supposed that later in the season, when colonies tend to become more prosperous, adult workers are more numerous and food is more plentiful, the female larvae receive more food and tend to develop into perfect females or queens.

The amount of food that any given larva receives obviously depends not only on the number of adult workers present in its colony to collect food, and distribute it, but also on the number of larvae being fed. Richards (1946) was the first person to measure the larva/worker ratio and, following his lead, Cumber studied this ratio in a number of colonies in different stages of development, and found that in colonies in which queens were being reared there was at least one worker for every larva; a considerably lower ratio than that usually found early on in the development of colonies. Thus this evidence lends support to the view that caste determination in female bumblebees is controlled by the quantity of food fed to the larvae.

However, Sladen (1912) originally held the view that an abundant food supply alone is insufficient to cause a female larva to develop into a queen, and thought it possible that queens can only be derived from eggs laid towards the end of a queen's life. Later he carried out an experiment in which he united two *B. latreillellus* colonies, without queens, together so that there were twenty workers to look after only three fertilised eggs. These eggs gave rise to females which he described as being "as large as queens". This was the first real experimental evidence in favour of the theory that queen-production depends upon a plentiful supply of food. However, although these three eggs were produced in two colonies which were only in the early stages of their development and it is unlikely that they would have developed into queens had the two colonies remained undisturbed, this possibility cannot be excluded. Similarly, the absence of a queen from this experimental colony may have affected the result. More recently both Cumber (1949a) and Free (1955a) have recorded instances in which queens have been produced in colonies much earlier than usual, following the deaths of the mother queens of the colonies concerned. In these cases, although loss of the mother queens probably led to a decrease in the larva/worker ratio and hence to a greater quantity of food becoming available per larva than would otherwise have been the case, it still remained possible that the determining factor, or at least a part of it, may have been the actual absence of the mother queens.

In order to investigate this problem further, Free started ten *B. pratorum* colonies in the laboratory by confining individual queens in company with various numbers of workers in nest-boxes in which plenty of honey and pollen was available. In five of the colonies female bees were eventually reared. In three of these five colonies the queens had to rear their brood either entirely on their own, or with the help of only a single worker, and only workers were produced in them. But in the other two colonies, one of which had two workers confined with the queen and the other five, queens as well as workers were produced from the first batches of eggs laid by their mother queens. It seems quite clear, therefore, that queen-production in a bumble-bee colony is governed by the number of workers available per larva, and that if sufficient workers and food are provided experimentally even the first batch of eggs will develop into queens, whereas under normal conditions, when the queen alone tends the larvae, they only give rise to workers.

The ratio of workers to larvae presumably governs within limits the quantity of food which each larva will receive, and, since bumblebees do not appear to produce any special glandular brood-food (p. 17), it seems unlikely that there are qualitative differences in the food supplied to queen and worker larvae respectively. Although both Sladen (1912) and Frison (1928) obtained data which suggest that the developmental stages of queens last longer than those of workers, it nevertheless seems improbable that the duration of these stages plays any important part in the rearing of queen bumblebees, since in Free's experiments the adult queens and workers emerged at about the same time.

The question now arises, how is this reduction in the larva/worker ratio brought about in nature? To answer this question we must refer once again to the work of Cumber. From his data he was able to estimate, by various methods, the egg-laying cycle of a queen—that is to say the number of eggs laid by her

Plate 7.—Details of Comb of *Bombus lucorum.* A
Egg-cells, apart from the first one, are always built by the queen herself on
top of cocoons.
above. A cell opened to expose eggs (x 2.5).
below. Group of young larvae exposed by removal of wax covering (x 2.5).

a

b

Plate 8.—Details of Comb of *Bombus lucorum*. B

As the larvae of a group grow older each becomes separated from its neighbours.

a. Group of cocoons and larvae. Some larvae can be seen in lower left-hand corner. An aperture is left in the wax covering each larva, through which it can be fed (x 1.2).

b. Group of cocoons, one of which has been cut open to show pupa (x 1.4).

every day throughout the whole of her life. He found that when he drew a graph showing the number of eggs laid each day the curve produced demonstrated that there is a marked reduction in the number of eggs laid by a queen prior to the production of sexual forms in her colony. This, of course, results in an increase in the number of workers available to care for each of the larvae present. We do not yet know, however, what factor causes a queen to lay unfertilised, male-producing eggs, nor do we know why they are laid in some colonies and not in others.

A complete range of size between small workers and large queens is found in the pocket-making species of bumblebees, and the reason for this is readily understood when we remember that, on account of the way in which the larvae are fed, there is considerable competition between them for the available food, and that some larvae are more favourably placed (in the larval batches) to obtain it than others (p. 19). Why is it, then, one may ask, that in the later stages of a colony's life only queens and no workers at all are produced by these pocket-making bees, since one would still expect some larvae to be placed so that they do not receive enough food? An observation by Plath (1934) may provide a clue to help answer this problem. He noted that in the American pocket-making species *B. impatiens* those larval groups whose members all become queens are fed solely on food *regurgitated* by the workers tending them, and that no pollen-pockets are formed. Furthermore, Free has recently successfully kept colonies of *B. agrorum* in confinement by providing them with honey and small balls of pollen (taken from honeybee colonies) placed a short distance from the comb, and, although under these circumstances wax pockets were formed on the larval groups, no pollen was placed in them; nevertheless the larvae appeared to develop normally, indicating that the workers were providing them with sufficient pollen by regurgitation alone. It appears probable, therefore, that in all the pocket-making species the diet of larvae destined to become queens is at least supplemented with pollen which is regurgitated to them by the workers, and so all the larvae receive sufficient food to develop into queens.

We noted earlier that there is a sharp distinction between the sizes of the workers and queens of those pollen-storing species whose larvae separate themselves from their neighbours early in their development and come to occupy individual cells (p. 28). This absence of intermediate forms is probably associated with the absence of any direct competition for food between the larvae. Apart from the reduction in the egg-laying rate of the queen, the amount of brood to be fed may also be reduced by the adult workers of colonies of these species actually destroying some of the eggs laid by their queen. However, we shall have more to say about this interesting activity later on (p. 59).

After the production of male and queen brood by a colony it never rears any new worker brood. Why this should be so is unknown. It is not, however, necessarily due to the old queen lacking sperm to fertilise any eggs she lays, since she may still have plenty in her sperm-storage organ (spermatheca). The appearance of the mother queen is now very different from when she came out of her winter quarters; not only are her wings tattered and torn, but much of the hair has been rubbed off her body leaving it black and shiny.

As the older worker bees die off there is a steady decline in the population of the colony, and, after the last adults have emerged, the queen and the few remaining worn-looking workers spend most of their time resting idly on top of the comb (Pl. 13a, p. 66). The nest temperature is no longer maintained at its previous high level and approaches that of the outside air, and, as the old queen and the last of her workers die off, decay and parasites of various kinds (Chapter 10, p. 87) get to work, and the old comb becomes derelict.

Before the colony dies out in this way any young queens it has produced will have mated and, after using the parental nest for a time, will disperse and burrow themselves into banks, or seek other sheltered places to wait for the spring—when it will be their turn to attempt to found new colonies of their own (see Chapter 5, p. 41). Only young impregnated queens survive the winter; the males, like the old mother queen and the workers, all die off before the winter begins.

Colonies of some of our species of bumblebees reach maturity, produce queens, and die out much earlier in the season than others. Thus males and young queens of our earliest nesting species, *B. pratorum*, may often be seen flying in May, and their colonies are probably all finished by the beginning of July.

Colonies of *B. agrorum,* on the other hand, may last well into September.

Some colonies contain smaller forces of workers at the time that queen larvae are produced than others of the same species, and consequently die out earlier in the season. The probable explanation for this is that these colonies are sited in places where the food-supply is particularly favourable and so are able to start to rear queens earlier, and with a smaller worker force, than larger colonies which are less favourably situated. An extreme example of the effect of an abundant food-supply on the time of onset of queen production has been provided by Richards (1927a) in his studies of bumblebees in the sub-artic. He found that, in correlation with the short prolific periods of plant growth and nectar secretion which occurs in that part of the world, the bumblebee colonies only produce a very few workers before beginning to rear queens.

Colony life-cycles also become modified to suit other climatic conditions. For example, in the warmer parts of New Zealand both males and queens have been seen on the wing at all times of the year, and queens found their nests at any time during some nine months (Cumber 1954). However, even though colonies may persist throughout a winter, they never return to the production of worker bees once they have reared queens.

Unfortunately we have comparatively little information about the habits of the few species of bumblebees which live in the tropics. It is known, however, that colony growth continues throughout the year, although it seems probable, from the observations made by Michener and Laberge (1954) in Mexico, that brood-production is greatly reduced during the dry season. In Brazil, von Ihering (1903) noted that fertilised queens and males sometimes overwinter in the parental nest, but his frequently quoted supposition that their colonies are perennial and multiply by swarming is now known to be incorrect; and Dias (1958) has reported that he has seen, in Brazil, individual bumblebee queens searching for nesting sites just as they do in this country.

In these first chapters we have now traced the life history of a bumblebee colony from the time it was founded in the spring by a single, overwintered, impregnated queen, through its development to maturity and the production of sexual forms, and so through its decline until all its members, other than the young queens, have died and the old nest has been abandoned to decay. In the following chapters we shall be more concerned with the activities of individual bees and will try to see how their behaviour becomes adapted to meet the needs of the social organisation of which they are a part.

Plate 9.—DETAILS OF COMB OF *Bombus lucorum*. C
Bumblebees store small quantities of food—pollen and honey—in their combs.
above. A group of pollen-storage cells (marked with arrows). The bee with
half-spread wings is depositing pollen in one of them (x 1·4).
below. Old cocoons are often used for the storage of honey (x 2·0).

Plate 10

CHAPTER 5

MALES AND YOUNG QUEENS

Then be not coy, but use your time,
And while ye may, go marry:
For having lost but once your prime,
You may for ever tarry.

ROBERT HERRICK. *To the Virgins,*
to make much of Time

MALE and queen bumblebees are only reared in colonies when they have reached a certain stage of prosperity; normally, several generations of workers are produced first. The average proportion of male to queen bumblebees is not known for certain, but Sladen's estimate that about twice as many males as queens are produced is probably near the mark. As we have seen (Chapter 4, p. 27) queens are more 'expensive' to rear than males, and no doubt the sex-ratio has become so adjusted that the maximum number of queens possible shall become fertilised.

Males do little to help in the economy of their colonies, and have never been seen to perform any work for them other than helping to incubate the brood. For the first few days of their lives they help themselves liberally to the honey and pollen

---

Plate 10 (opposite). *Bombus agrorum*—A POCKET-MAKING SPECIES
above. General view of comb. Cocoons which arise from each egg batch tend to form distinct groups. Three groups can be seen and the queen is on the group on the right hand side (x 1·7)
below. A pocket in which pollen is deposited is attached to each larval group. One in the centre is marked (x). An egg clump is present on top of a cocoon on the left hand side (Y). (x 2·7)

BB—D

stores in their nests. If their colony is disturbed they tend to hide themselves beneath the comb or in the nesting material.

Free marked a large number of males of several species as soon as they had emerged, and found that most of them flew from their nests when they were between two and four days old, whereas both queens and workers are usually older before they fly. Once these males had left their nests they were never seen to return to them again. However, it is evident that the males of certain species do sometimes return (Frison, 1917 and 1928), but even these males soon desert their nests for good. Males that have left their nests collect their own food (Pl. 20b, p. 115) and take shelter, at night and in inclement weather, wherever they can.

In contrast to males, young queens may carry out all kinds of household duties in the nests in which they were reared, including feeding of the brood, and they sometimes even produce wax and help the workers to defend their colonies (Frison 1928). Thirty *B. lucorum* queens observed by Free first flew when they were between two and eight days old, and several of them foraged for their maternal colony, collecting both nectar and pollen. The extent to which young queens perform these duties may perhaps depend on the needs of their colonies at the time, and in colonies that have become short of workers the activities of the young queens may help to rear the final batches of brood. The important events at this stage of a young queen's life are, however, her fertilisation and her preparations for hibernation.

It seems to be true of all species of bumblebees that during copulation the male mounts upon the back of the female and grips the tip of her abdomen with a pair of claspers at the tip of his own. In contrast to the difficulties which beekeepers have experienced when they have tried to induce queen honeybees to mate in captivity, the mating of bumblebee queens can readily be induced merely by confining young queens and males together in a small container. Males and queens of several British and American species have been induced to mate in this way, the two sexes often remaining *in coitu* for long periods.

Frison (1927a) mentions that his queens sometimes attacked the males he placed with them; but that he was occasionally able to overcome this difficulty by substituting further males for those which seemed to be unacceptable to the queens. Some males appeared indifferent to the queens with whom they were confined; and he found that males which had been segregated from queens ever since they had emerged from their cells, were more likely to attempt to mate when they were subsequently placed with them, than were other males who had been kept continuously with queens; Free even found that *B. pratorum* males which had been isolated attempted to copulate with worker bumblebees when the latter were confined with them.

As with many other activities, the different species of bumblebees differ widely in their mating habits. The males of some species, e.g. *B. latreillellus* and *B. ruderarius*, hover around the entrances of nests of their own species and wait for young queens to come out, whereupon they attempt to seize them and mate with them. Males of these species can also sometimes be seen to dart down towards workers as they leave their nests, though they do not attempt to seize them. This suggests that it is perhaps her scent that actually causes a male bumblebee to seize a queen, and that he has to approach fairly closely to her before he can appreciate her distinctive odour. It would certainly be interesting to study this question, and also to determine whether males usually linger close to the entrances of the nests in which they were reared waiting for the queens, their sisters, to come out; or whether they always seek out the nests of other colonies: in other words, to try to discover how often brother-sister mating takes place.

Sometimes males that have been hovering round the entrance to a nest have been seen to chase queens down the entrance tunnel, and it seems quite possible that they may have caught and mated with them in the nest itself. Copulation often takes place between males and queens whose colonies are confined in the laboratory, and it has also been seen to occur between members of a colony of *B. pratorum* housed in a nest-box from which the bees were able to fly at will (Pl. 12a, p. 51), but it is impossible to say how often this occurs in nature.

Males of other species also lie in wait for queens, but not around the entrances to their nests. Each selects an object such as a flower, fencepost or rock, and remains close to it for hours on end, sometimes hovering slowly in the air, and at others standing almost motionless and very alert, with antennae held erect and wings half spread, as though lurking for prey. When a queen bumblebee or other large insect—or even a bird—flies past, the male leaves his observation post and darts after it, chasing it until he either captures a mate or discovers that the object is not a nubile queen. In the latter case he returns again to his observation post to wait once more for a queen to come along. The males of those species that exhibit this behaviour, e.g. *B. confusus* (Radl, quoted by von Buttel-Reepen 1903), *B. mendax* (Saunders 1909), *B. auricomus*, *B. morrisoni* and *B. separatus* (Frison 1917 and 1930), possess enormous eyes and Richards, (1927b) points out that differences in the relative sizes of the eyes of males and females are characteristic of insect species in which 'marriage by capture' is the rule. However, even the possession of such well-developed eyes does not lead to ready recognition of a female at a distance. The males will chase any creature about the size of a queen bumblebee, and, if a stone is thrown into the air near a waiting male he will dart after it and pursue it to the ground. This behaviour seems to suggest once again that males are only able to recognise queens with certainty when they are very close to them.

Perhaps the most fascinating behaviour of all, and certainly that which has attracted most attention of late, is shown by the males of certain species, such as *B. hypnorum* and *B. terrestris*, who fly along established routes in a seemingly endless procession, momentarily hovering every now and then at special places along them. Early observers noted that the places visited, which may range from a spot at the base of a tree or shrub to a small twig or single leaf, smell very similar to the males themselves, and suggested that nubile queens are attracted to the vicinity of these places where the males find them and mating occurs.

The first careful study of these flight paths was made by Frank (1941), who marked males with spots of paint and found that individuals always fly in one definite direction and, furthermore, since they returned every few minutes to the place that he was observing, he concluded that they must fly in a circuit. One particular *B. hypnorum* male which he observed flew round his route as many as 77 times on a rather overcast day; and another male, a *B. terrestris*, completed his circuit 35 times in 90 minutes. The length of the complete flight route of this

B. terrestris male was about 275 metres (300 yds.) and contained 27 visiting places which were mostly between 5 and 15 metres (5—16 yds.) apart, but sometimes as little as 30 or 40 centimetres (12—16 ins.). The greatest distance between any two of the places was 33 metres (36 yds.). Frank calculated that during 10 hours of flight, which it is quite possible for a bumblebee to make on a favourable day, this male would have flown as much as 60 kilometres (37 miles). The lengths of the flight routes of different males varied, of course; small weak males appeared generally to have shorter circuits than larger, stronger ones. The only times that males were seen to deviate from their route was when they sought nourishment from nearby flowers, although on a cool day they would sometimes rest in sunny places for a few minutes.

Although each male followed his own particular route, the routes of various males overlapped and several visiting places were held in common, so that in a given area there was in effect a network of interwoven routes along which the males flew in all directions, and, during favourable weather, scarcely a minute went by without at least one male arriving at each of the established visiting places. The flight routes of individual males were not static, however, but varied slightly from day to day, certain visiting places along them being discarded and others incorporated.

The work of Frank was followed by that of Hass (1946 and HAAS ? 1952), who discovered that males scent-mark the visiting places only once a day, first thing in the morning. This daily marking of the route accounts for the fact that males will desert some of the points visited on the previous day and include new ones. When laying down the scent the males grip the leaves, twigs or pieces of bark they are scent-marking in their mandibles and make gnawing movements, often simultaneously whirring their wings in an excited manner. The scent is apparently produced from glands at the bases of their mandibles and secreted onto the leaf or other object chosen and so 'marks' it. Kullenberg (1956) noticed that the scent produced by *B. hortorum* males smells very similar to hydroxycitronellal; when he placed some of this substance on small areas of the trunks and branches of trees he found that males of this species were actually attracted.

Male bumblebees apparently produce scents which are

characteristic of their own particular species, and this undoubtedly helps to account for the fact that only members of the same species use the same visiting places. Different species also make their flight-routes in different sorts of places, and Hass (1949a) *Haas* found he could group species according to the height above ground level at which their members established flight-paths. Males of one group, exemplified by *B. lapidarius*, regularly fly at treetop level, others, e.g. *B. agrorum, B. pratorum* and *B. sylvarum*, at the level of bushes or shrubs, others, e.g. *B. pomorum* and *B. terrestris* at the level of herbage, and still others, e.g. *B. hypnorum*, have their flight-paths nearly at ground level. Even within one locality there may be noticeable differences in the levels at which the males of the different species fly. However, the behaviour of the males is flexible enough to meet current circumstances, and species whose flight-paths are normally established at treetop level will, in regions where there are no trees, make do with routes closer to the ground (Krüger, 1951).

Males of the genus *Psithyrus*, the parasitic bumblebees (Chapter 9, p. 71), also fly along predetermined courses (Hass, 1949b), although, in the case of *P. silvestris* at any rate, the flight-paths are not marked by a series of visiting points but by areas a few feet square, the *Psithyrus* males flying a zig-zag course within each area before proceeding straight to the next one.

There can be little doubt that the biological function of these flight-routes of male bumblebees is to ensure that any nubile queen of the same species who enters the mosaic of flight paths quickly finds a mate. Frison (1927a) was the first person to study the reactions of males towards queens on a flight-route. He suspended young queens by thread from the branches of trees and bushes along a route, but, although males were attracted to these queens he never saw mating take place. Better results were obtained by Cumber (1953) who tethered three *B. pratorum* queens along a flight-path used by *B. pratorum* males. All three queens were quickly found by males who mated with them, one pair remaining in copula for nearly $1\frac{1}{2}$ hours.

Minderhoud in Holland has recently investigated the behaviour of *B. agrorum* males towards dead queens which he pinned down at one of their scenting places along a flight-route. One particular *B. agrorum* queen was preferred to all the others, and several males mounted her, one male even trying, on more than one occasion, to mate with her. This queen had been dead for seven weeks when these observations were made and when she was once again placed on a flight-path the next year, by which time she had been dead for nearly fourteen months, a male mounted her and persisted for three minutes in trying to copulate with her! Why this particular dead queen was more attractive than others it is difficult to imagine, and we must await further results with interest.

Many questions concerning the mating behaviour of bumble-bees still remain unanswered. We do not know if the queens mate once only, or whether they usually mate with more than one male, as has recently been shown to be the case in the honeybee. We do not even know at what age males become sexually mature, or whether they are able to mate more than once or die soon after mating for the first time.

During the time that the young queens remain attached to their maternal colonies they frequently help themselves to the stored food, and the size of their fat-bodies increases greatly to form their food-reserves during hibernation. Pollen, as well as honey, is eaten by the young queens; any dissected 24 hours after they have emerged from their cocoons are found to have large quantities in their alimentary canals.

It seems that the ability of young queens to store up food-reserves within their bodies—an ability that workers do not possess to anything like the same extent—is not dependent on previous fertilisation, since the fat-bodies of newly emerged *B. pratorum* queens which Free confined together for a month became as large as those of fertilised queens. Although fertilisation is not a necessary prelude to fat-body development, it may perhaps cause physiological changes to occur which enable queens to survive the winter, since Cumber (1954) found that all the queens he dissected in spring were fertilised.

When they have mated, and their fat-bodies have developed, the queens eventually fill their honey-stomachs and go into their winter quarters. It is not known whether queens find the places in which they are going to hibernate before they finally leave their maternal nests; nor do we know how long it usually takes a queen to discover a suitable place. Perhaps each queen returns to her maternal nest each evening until she has found a suitable site. The onset of hibernation is certainly not governed by temperature since young queens of some species (e.g. *B. pratorum*) enter their winter quarters at the height of summer and in this respect the word 'hibernation' which is derived from the Latin word 'hibernare' meaning 'to pass the winter', is somewhat misleading. However, in spring the time at which queens reappear does seem to be determined by temperature.

We really possess very little information about the hibernating habits of queen bumblebees. In the tropics both males and fertilised young queens have been reported by von Ihering (1903) to pass the unfavourable season in their maternal nests. In temperate regions queens have been found hibernating beneath moss, dead leaves, straw and other matted vegetation and also in burrows in the ground, and Skovgaard (1945) reports that in Denmark many queens hibernate in the cavities of stone walls.

Queens of different species probably choose different kinds of places in which to hibernate; thus Sladen (1912) has stated that *B. terrestris* queens bury themselves in the soil under trees whilst *B. lapidarius* queens burrow a few inches into the soil of well-drained banks. He found that the banks which queens chose mostly faced north or north-west and pointed out that queens hibernating in banks with these aspects were unlikely to be awakened prematurely by the warmth of the winter sun. He found many *B. lapidarius* queens hibernating in such banks, and noted that the position of each queen was marked by a heap of fine earth, at the entrance of her burrow, which the rain eventually washed away.

Plath (1934) gives an interesting account of how he discovered that young *B. impatiens* queens often hibernate within a few feet of the entrances to the nests in which they were reared; on one occasion he saw forty of them digging themselves into the soil around their old home. As a result of his discoveries, he suggested that the concentrations of queens that Sladen had discovered in banks probably arose because they were hibernating close to their old nests. Since Plath made his observations, however, Bols (1937) of Belgium has published observations which definitely show that large concentrations of hibernating queens occur in suitable sites which are not close to the nests in which these queens were reared. These hibernating sites were steep sandy banks covered with plants and with a north-west exposure, and in them he found queens of several species of bumblebees of the genus *Psithyrus*, as well as of the genus *Bombus*, hibernating close together. Each queen was situated in her own separate chamber, which was spherical and about the size of a walnut and some 4-5 inches below ground level, and lay on her back with her wings folded. Bols was able to observe the behaviour of a *P. vestalis* from the time of her arrival at the hibernating site. First she pushed aside the moss covering the soil and then began to dig a burrow in the space that she had cleared. At first the soil she dug out formed a ring around the entrance, but as she went deeper the burrow became filled in behind her with the soil she was excavating, and, after half an hour, she was completely hidden from view.

To date, observations on the hibernating habits of only a few species of bumblebees have been made, and much still requires to be found out before we can obtain a truly representative picture of where the queens of all our different species hibernate.

Attempts have been made from time to time to cause bumblebee queens to hibernate under semi-natural conditions. In their experiments both Sladen (1912) and Frison (1927a) first of all confined the young queens they captured with males, in the hope that any of them which had not mated would do so. Sladen's queens (*B. lapidarius*) were kept in cages, the floors of which were covered with moss or loose soil, but none of them hibernated successfully. Frison originally tried wintering queens in tins containing loose soil and dried leaves but met only with failure. He ultimately obtained most success (the precise degree of success is not clear from his remarks) by keeping the queens he had collected in small perforated cardboard tubes, which he then placed in a large glass jar with a perforated lid and buried about a foot below the surface of the ground.

Plath dug up queens of *B. impatiens* he found hibernating, and confined one group in a box with six inches of soil on the bottom, and another group in a cage that was partly sunk into the soil. Even with these queens that were collected whilst they were hibernating little success was achieved, none of the first group surviving the winter and only 10 per cent of the second.

The small degree of success obtained in these attempts to winter queens in captivity suggests that they require special conditions if they are to hibernate successfully, and it may perhaps be the nature of their requirements that results in queens hibernating in numbers in favourable places.

The best method yet devised for overwintering queens in captivity seems to be that devised by Cumber (1953). He captured his queens either on the wing as they returned to their maternal colonies, or opened their nests and collected those that flew out. He then placed each in a separate tube, an inch in diameter, and put a small piece of muslin over a hole which he had bored through its cork to ensure adequate ventilation. On returning to his laboratory he removed the corks and inverted the tubes over a special feeding tray containing a mixture of honey and water and allowed each queen 15 minutes to feed. He then replaced the corks and stored the queens in their tubes in a dark cellar at about 15°C. (59°F.). On each of the following three days the queens were again fed and after that they were given food twice a week for several weeks. On 12th January just over half of the queens he had kept since October were still alive. He dissected thirty of them and found that all but two had been fertilised and that their fat-bodies were well developed and typical of those of hibernating queens. Unfortunately, he was unable to continue this interesting experiment to see what proportion would have remained alive until the spring. An advantage of this method of overwintering queens in captivity is that they cannot become infected with the parasitic nematode worm *Sphaerularia bombi* which so frequently attacks hibernating queens under natural conditions.

It is only by continuing with studies such as these that we shall acquire further information on the conditions necessary for the successful overwintering of bumblebee queens.

CHAPTER 6

THE DIVISION OF LABOUR
IN A COLONY

The bee is more honoured than other animals,
not because she labours, but because she labours
for others.

ST JOHN CHRYSOSTOM. *Homilies*

THE efficiency of a social group is increased if the various tasks
essential to its well-being are divided amongst the individuals
of which it is composed, and the question therefore arises as to
whether any such division of labour exists between the workers
of a bumblebee colony. As long ago as 1890 Coville noted that
in a bumblebee colony workers of different sizes often perform
different tasks. Whilst studying a colony of *B. borealis* he noticed
that it was the larger bees that went foraging and manipulated
the nesting material surrounding the comb, whilst the smaller
bees for the most part carried out tasks inside the nest.

It was not, however, until more than fifty years later that any
definite evidence of a division of labour among the bumblebees
of a colony, on the basis of size, became available, when, in 1946,
Richards published the results of his observations. He collected
three colonies of *B. agrorum* and classified the bees either as house-
bees or as foragers according to whether he found them in the
nest or collected them as they returned to it from foraging. He
found that in each colony the foragers tended to be the larger and
suggested that body-size may perhaps form the basis of a real
division of labour among the workers of bumblebee colonies.
Since then Cumber (1949a) has measured the size of the house-
bees and foragers in several colonies, and it has now been well
established that a division of labour on the basis of size occurs

amongst the workers in colonies of most, if not all, species of bumblebees.

Other people have studied the division of labour between the members of colonies by making careful observations of the behaviour of individuals whose colonies were housed in special observation nest-boxes fitted with glass roofs. All the bees in these colonies were given distinctive paint-marks, so that each could be recognised and her behaviour recorded. Meidell (1934) gives an interesting account of a *B. agrorum* colony he studied in this way. He found that individual bees seemed to prefer certain duties, some spending much of their time foraging whilst others mostly occupied themselves with house duties. For some days after a bee first began to forage she did so only intermittently, spending much of her time inside the nest; later, however, she developed into a typical forager and spent a great deal of her life in the field.

Brian (1952) and Free (1955b), who also observed the behaviour of marked bees, weighed each of the bees of the colonies with which they were working to obtain information on the activities of bees of different sizes. Brian was able to show that in colonies of *B. agrorum* the distinction between the behaviour of large and small workers lies not in any clear-cut permanent division of duties, but rather in the age at which the bees of these two groups took up work in the field. In general the small workers did not begin to forage until they were older than the larger ones, so that on any one day the average size of the foragers was greater than that of the bees remaining inside the nest. Some of the smallest workers in Brian's colonies never went foraging at all, however, whereas other observers have recorded two-day-old bees returning to their nests with loads of pollen.

Free classified the bees in his colonies either as consistent foragers, if they went out on seventy per cent. or more of the days on which the activities of members of their colonies were recorded, or as consistent house-bees if they were never seen to leave their nests. Over periods of a few days he found that most bees were either consistent foragers or consistent house-bees, but that about a third of the population of a colony was not constant to either duty. Even in cases of very small colonies, containing only a queen and three or four workers, a division of labour was apparent, one or two of the bees never leaving the nest and the others acting as foragers.

Although the average size of the foragers of a colony is greater than that of the house-bees, a few of the relatively larger bees in Free's colonies were never seen to go foraging at all and, conversely, some of the tiny bees did go out foraging. Analysis of the data obtained showed that the smaller bees that went foraging did so less regularly than their larger sisters. We still do not know the reason why smaller bees often never go foraging at all, or, if they do, start later in life than their larger sisters and even then are less persistent foragers.

Of what biological importance is such a division of labour, based on the size of its workers, to a bumblebee colony? Two advantages can be immediately suggested. Firstly, it is clear that the smaller workers must be able to move more easily through the intricate galleries of the comb than their larger sisters, and thus are better suited to perform household duties; the larger bees, on the other hand, are able to collect greater loads of nectar and pollen and, one would suppose, may also be able to fly when conditions are less favourable.

In order that a social unit may function efficiently it is necessary that the division of labour among its members shall not be too rigid or it may defeat its own ends. In the case of bumblebee colonies, if the foraging force becomes depleted by adverse weather conditions it is necessary that it should be reinforced by bees who would otherwise be carrying out household duties, if the colony is to obtain sufficient food. The question is, therefore, whether the division of labour in a bumblebee colony is sufficiently adaptable to meet such demands. In the first place several observers have noted that late in the summer tiny bumblebee workers are sometimes to be seen foraging, and it has been suggested that these workers would probably have been acting as house-bees had they belonged to prosperous colonies but, because their colonies had passed their peaks of strength and were now rapidly dwindling, they were compelled to go out to replace the older foragers who had already died. But it could also be argued that these tiny workers had only just become sufficiently old to start foraging and would have done so irrespective of the needs of their colonies.

Free (1955b) has carried out experiments with several colonies to see whether house-bees will take over the duties of foragers if it becomes desirable for the economy of their colonies. First he observed each colony for several days to find out which bees were consistent foragers and which were house-bees, and he then removed several or all of its foragers and placed them in a cage in the laboratory. The colony was then watched for the next few days to see whether any of the house-bees would take over the duties of the missing field-bees. In each experiment it was found that several of the house-bees, who had in all probability never been foraging in their lives before, began to do so in the absence of the normal foragers. Indeed, after the foragers had been removed from a small *B. lapidarius* colony even the queen started to forage again! In other cases bees that had been amongst the less consistent foragers undertook many more trips than before. When the foragers who had been taken away were returned to these colonies it was found that the original house-bees tended to give up foraging and to revert once more to their former duties inside the nest.

Having found by experiment that house-bees will augment the field force when necessary for the well-being of their colony, attempts were made to find out if the converse is also true— whether some of the foragers of a colony will stay inside their nest and look after the brood if for some reason the nursing force becomes depleted.

A similar series of experiments to those mentioned above were performed, but this time some of the house-bees were removed instead of some of the foragers. The results were not as consistent as those obtained when foragers were removed, but it seems safe to conclude from them that if the household force had been fully occupied before some of its members were removed then some of the foragers stayed inside their nest and reinforced the depleted nursing population, although it took the bees a day or two to readjust themselves. Those bees who had previously only been inconsistent foragers were found to become full-time household bees more readily than others who had been spending much of their time foraging, although some of these also adapted themselves to household duties. Perhaps these were bees who had only recently begun to forage. If on the other hand, after some of the house-bees had been removed, the reduced household force was apparently still adequate to look after the brood, then the majority of the foragers still continued to collect food. In such cases it appeared that there had previously been more house-bees present than the colony actually required, and that so long as sufficient food was being brought into the nest these redundant house-bees did not forage.

The results of these experiments lead one to ask: why is it that some bees more readily adapt themselves to their colonies' needs than others? Perhaps there is some relationship between the length of time a bee has been performing a particular duty and her tendency to continue to do so. In a final experiment, Free started a colony by confining captured foragers in a nest-box, together with a queen and brood from another colony. After three weeks further strange bees, newly captured while foraging, were added and, two days later, the entrance to the nest-box was opened so that the bees could fly. The colony was now observed for the next few days, and it was found that those bees who had recently been added to the colony foraged much more than those which had been confined for over three weeks. This result definitely suggests that the longer an individual bee has been carrying out either household or foraging activities, the greater her tendency to continue with whatever activity she has hitherto been concerned. Incidentally, this is, of course, likely to be advantageous to their colonies since bees that have been foraging most recently will presumably already know the best nectar and pollen sources in the vicinity.

We see, then, that the behaviour of the workers of a bumble-bee colony results in an efficient division of labour between them, in which each individual, although she tends to remain either a forager or a household bee for days on end, can, and will if needs be, do whatever task is necessary to meet her colony's requirements.

So far we have only been concerned with a division of labour between house-bees and foragers. But in the case of a honeybee colony a much more elaborate division of labour exists and there is a tendency for each bee to perform a sequence of duties within the hive as she grows older, although this sequence is often greatly modified to suit her colony's day-to-day requirements.

Does a worker bumblebee follow any similar sequence of duties?

Much of the time of a house-bee of a bumblebee colony is spent in incubating the brood, interspersed with such activities as producing and manipulating wax, feeding larvae and arranging nest-material. Meidell (1934) found that even during the first day of her adult life a worker takes part in the work of her colony to some extent and may perhaps clean out some empty cocoons ready for food to be stored in them. He also mentions that at such an early age she spends a good deal of time helping to incubate the brood. By the time a worker is two or three days old, however, she is performing all the necessary household tasks. Jordan (1936) who observed a small colony of *B. muscorum* found that during the first 3-4 days of their lives the bees confined their activities to consuming food and cleaning out cells, but, thereafter, they apparently undertook any nest duty that required attention.

On the other hand Verlaine (1934) claimed that workers may feed larvae, manipulate wax, and take part in building operations, when they are one day old or less. But even if this does sometimes happen, it is improbable that workers secrete wax during the first day or two of their lives, since Frison (1917) has pointed out that he has never seen wax being produced by workers whose coats have not yet developed their full colouration.

Brian was unable to detect any particular trend in the duties undertaken by her bees as they grew older, although she did mention that certain bees might be seen doing the same tasks, such as fanning or rearranging the nesting material, day after day; she suggested that this was largely a matter of habit.

Late in the development of their colony certain bees, especially the house-bees, may become egg-layers—but we will consider their activities in the next chapter.

Plate 11 (opposite). BUMBLEBEE NESTS

above. B. *pratorum*—a pollen-storing species. This colony has reached maturity and has already reared some males (bottom left hand side) and young queens (bee at top centre). Note shiny, hairless thorax of old mother queen (on right hand side of comb). (x 1·3)

below. B. *ruderarius*—a pocket-making species. Note queen on group of cocoons on right hand side, and newly emerged worker in centre (x 2.3)

Plate 11

a

b

*Plate 12.—Bombus pratorum—*MALES AND YOUNG QUEENS

a. Side view of mature colony showing males and young queens. A pair on lower left-hand side of comb are copulating. A male is flying away. Once a male has left his maternal nest he seldom, if ever, returns to it again (x 1·0).

b. Male and young queen mating—they may remain in this position for several hours (x 3·1).

A careful study of the activities of individual house-bees might well be rewarding, as little is known about how often the larvae are fed and whether some house-bees feed them more often than others. Several observers have noticed that when foragers are in their nests for any length of time they too may carry out all kinds of household tasks. Do they tend, however, to keep more to such tasks as wax manipulation, and to leave duties such as feeding the brood to the house-bees?

A word must now be said about the longevity of worker bumblebees. Jordan found that his *B. muscorum* workers lived from 5-8 weeks, but Brian found that about half of her bees (*B. agrorum*) were dead within 3 weeks of emergence, although some of them lived for more than 60 days, the house-bees tending to live longer than the foragers. She associated the tendency of a field-bee to die earlier than a house-bee to the bad weather conditions with which a forager often has to contend, and she noted that foragers lived longer during 1947, a favourable season, than they did in 1948 when the weather was frequently bad.

Later (Chapter 11, p. 93) we will consider the division of labour amongst the foragers and discuss whether the food they collect bears any relationship to the needs of their colonies.

CHAPTER 7

EGG-LAYING WORKERS

For among Bees and Ants are social systems found
so complex and well-order'd as to invite offhand
a pleasant fable enough: that once upon a time,
or ever a man was born to rob their honeypots,
bees were fully endow'd with Reason and only lost it
by ordering so their life as to dispense with it;
whereby it pined away and perish'd of disuse.

ROBERT BRIDGES. *The Testament of Beauty*

STRUCTURALLY worker and queen bumblebees differ from one another mainly in size and the ovaries of workers usually remain in the form of thin threads—similar to those of a queen before she hibernates. Under some conditions, however, the ovaries of workers develop and they may lay eggs. Such worker-produced eggs are usually smaller than those laid by queens and, being unfertilised, give rise to males. At one time it was supposed that these egg-laying workers had previously mated but this idea has long since been discredited.

The construction of egg-cells and the laying of eggs by workers may take place in a colony at about the time it reaches maturity and the first males and queens are emerging, although ovary development in workers also often occurs if the mother queen of the colony becomes lost or is removed at an earlier stage in its history.

When egg-laying workers are present in a colony the usual state of harmony no longer prevails, and many students of bumblebee behaviour have witnessed the hostility shown by the queen to such workers, and also between the workers themselves. For example Frison (1917) remarked that at such times the workers "were abnormally irritable, frequently biting one another". Such behaviour is more common in the case of some species than of others.

Recently Free (1955c) studied such antagonistic behaviour, and found that if he removed the queen from a colony, or made up a colony artificially by confining a small number of foragers, which he had caught in the field, together in a nest-box, the workers started to quarrel among themselves within a day or two. In each of these colonies, however, one of the workers appeared to adopt the status of a queen and to dominate the others. When disturbed she would beat her wings in an agitated manner, which was very reminiscent of that of a 'broody' queen (p. 168).

This 'dominant' individual would spend most of her time astride a new egg-cell, the eggs in which she herself had probably laid, and when another bee came too close she would open her mandibles and butt her head against the intruder, who nearly always retreated passively. A dominant bee rarely actually bit an intruder, and then only if her supremacy was contested. Often there was another bee present in the colony who would attack any bee except the dominant one. This second dominant individual was herself the favourite target for the dominant bee's attacks, and this dominant bee would sometimes pursue the second dominant one, constantly butting her, until she had chased her away from the egg-clump. Less frequently there would be a third dominant bee present who would attack any bee apart from the first and second dominant ones. Thus we find in effect, a simple form of hierarchical organisation based solely on the dominance of one or more bees over the others, similar in many respects to the peck-order found in some groups of birds. Not all dominance orders were found to be as simple as this, however, and, in large colonies especially, more complicated situations sometimes occurred for a while. Thus, for example, although bee X might dominate bee Y, and Y in her turn dominate bee Z, Z in some cases was found to dominate X. This sort of thing also occurs among birds.

Aggressive behaviour was at its maximum in a colony at about the time that the first eggs were laid by workers, and thereafter it slowly declined until by about a week later all visible signs of quarrelling had disappeared. However, considerable numbers of attacks were made before any eggs at all had been laid, so it seems that the aggressive behaviour of dominant worker bees is not solely dependent on the actual presence of egg-clumps.

After observations had been made, all the bees were dissected and the degree of development of their ovaries was measured. In many a colony the ovaries of its dominant bee were the most highly developed, and those of its second dominant the next most highly developed, so it seems probable that the aggressive behaviour displayed by a dominant bee is correlated with the large size of her ovaries.

Once an hierarchy had become established in a colony it did not remain constant indefinitely; sometimes a change in the dominance order would occur. Such changes appeared to be associated with the development of the ovaries and the laying of eggs by another worker who was thus stimulated to become aggressive towards the others, and possibly also with a regression in the degree of ovary development of the previous dominant. It was fascinating to watch a change in the dominance order taking place. Instead of passively retreating when attacked by the previous dominant bee the worker with the newly developed ovaries would challenge her in turn, and often they would fight ferociously for several seconds until one or other gave way.

On several occasions the dominant bee of one colony was introduced experimentally to the workers of another queenless colony. If, just before this was done, the dominant bee of the recipient colony was removed, then the introduced bee established her dominance in nearly every case. If, on the other hand, the dominant bee of the recipient colony was still present then she and the introduced dominant bee would always single each other out for attack. Apart from the usual butting attacks, they would attempt to bite and to clasp each other as if endeavouring to sting, although they never actually did so. Within a few minutes, however, one of them would break off the engagement and acknowledge defeat by retiring to a corner of the nest-box where she sometimes lay huddled up with her abdominal segments contracted. In most cases the bee who won the conflict was the one who was fighting in her own nest. When the dominant bees who had been introduced to strange colonies were once more reintroduced to their own colonies their status in them depended on the result of the conflicts they had fought in the strange colonies. If a bee had been dominant in the strange colony she invariably became dominant when returned to her own; but, if, on the other hand, she had been beaten in her conflict in the strange colony she was nearly always dominated by the second dominant on being returned to her own colony. It seems obvious, therefore, that psychological factors are the immediate determiners of the social status of a bee in one of these queenless colonies, and may themselves be affected by physiological causes.

It became apparent during this work that at least some of the members of a social order are able to recognise each other as individuals. Thus, as we have seen, the dominant bee of a colony selects for attack the second most dominant bee of her own colony, or a dominant bee which has been introduced from another colony, and bees whose ovaries are only slightly developed receive few attacks. It is conceivable that dominant bees recognised other dominant bees that had been introduced from other colonies by their strange colony odour (Chapter 8, p. 66), but this could not be the means by which they distinguish the second most dominant bees from the remaining bees in their own colonies. In many cases a dominant bee would attack the second most dominant when they met on a part of the comb other than that in which eggs were present, and appeared to be able to recognise her even though she did not seem to be behaving any differently from other bees. When we consider the capabilities of insect sense organs it seems probable that scent must form the basis of this recognition, and it seems most likely that the scent of a female bumblebee is associated in some way with the degree of development of her ovaries.

If, instead of a dominant worker, a vigorous queen is introduced to a queenless colony in which a social order exists, she, like a dominant worker from another colony, is immediately attacked by the dominant worker of the recipient colony. However, in contrast to the outcome of conflicts between dominant workers, in practically every case the queen eventually establishes her dominance and, during the next day or so, can be seen to attack the workers. It may be that the larger size of the queen may help her to establish her supremacy, and her much larger ovaries may also help to determine her greater aggressiveness. However, a few days after a queen has been introduced into a small queenless colony peace prevails once again and there are no signs of animosity. Queens, like dominant workers, can lose their dominant status in a colony. Thus in one colony under observation some of the workers attacked their queen, who had previously been dominant, whenever she climbed onto the comb. The next day she had an injured leg and was trying to escape from the nest-box, and two days later she was dead. Such loss of dominant status by a queen probably seldom occurs until shortly before her colony dies out.

Although most of the above investigations were conducted with B. pratorum, similar behaviour occurred when B. agrorum and B. lucorum workers were confined without queens, so that it seems likely that it is common to all species.

We have dealt rather extensively with the behaviour of laying workers because, as we shall see, this behaviour is important in enabling us to postulate how the social organisation of a bumblebee colony is maintained.

We have noted that the ovaries of the workers of a bumblebee colony usually develop at the time that the sexual brood is produced, or earlier if their queen is removed. Why does ovary development occur in workers at these times and not at others? Many years ago Wheeler postulated that the worker castes of social insects are produced by the undernourishment of larvae and he also suggested that exhausting labour on slender rations tends to keep adult workers sterile and to prevent their ovaries from developing. Let us examine this latter part of Wheeler's theory to see how it fits in with what we know about ovary development in worker bumblebees.

Several investigators (e.g. Richards 1946; Cumber 1949a) have found that when workers with developed ovaries are present in a colony, they are to be found more commonly amongst the house-bees than among the foragers. These findings appear to agree quite well with Wheeler's theory, as it is to be expected that house-bees live less strenuously than foragers, and we find that they also tend to possess better developed ovaries. However, the relatively greater length of life of house-bees (Brian 1952) and consequently greater time available for their ovaries to develop, possibly contributes to this result. At about the stage of colony growth at which workers normally begin to lay eggs, there is probably plenty of food in the nest as a result of the low larva/worker ratio which prevails at this time (Chapter 4, p. 30); similarly, if the queen of a colony dies prematurely there will again be a reduction in the amount of brood to be fed and cared for, which will result in a surplus of food and the necessity for less work to be done by each worker bee.

We may then tentatively conclude that the presence of plenty of food, together with lack of strenuous activity, is one of the factors in the development of the ovaries of worker bees. However, there may be no egg-laying workers present in colonies which possess considerable reserves of food (Cumber 1949a) indicating that other factors are of prime importance.

Recently Free (1957) discovered that the development of a worker's ovaries can be influenced both by the number of bees present together, and also by the temperature of their environment. He captured a large number of foraging bumblebees and confined them for a week in small cages, in each of which there was a small ball of pollen and a feeder containing sugar syrup. Some of the bees were kept in solitary confinement, others in pairs, still others in groups of five or ten. It was found that, in general, the degree of ovary development of the workers concerned was correlated with the number confined together. In several of the cages eggs were laid. Although some solitary workers laid eggs, relatively more eggs were present in cages containing the larger numbers of workers. The exact cause of the effect of this group stimulation on ovary development is not known, but, by analogy with studies that have been made on other animal species, including rats, birds and fish, one may suppose that the presence of other individuals stimulates a worker bee to eat more food and thus to obtain the necessary nourishment for ovary development to occur. The cages of bees were divided into three groups which were kept at room temperature, at 28°C. (82°F.), and at 32°C. (90°F.) respectively. The ovaries of those bees who were kept singly, or in groups of two or five individuals, at room temperature did not develop to the same extent as those kept in equivalent numbers at higher temperatures. However, the sizes of the ovaries of bees kept in groups of ten at these different temperatures was about the same, so that it appears that the retarding influence of low temperature on ovary development was balanced in these cases by the presence of ten bees together, probably because a group of this size caused a sufficient rise in their temperature.

At about the time that laying workers usually appear in a colony the temperature of the nest has become relatively stable at about 30°C. to 34°C. (86°—93°F.) (Himmer 1933 and Cumber 1949a) and the population is at its maximum. As we have just seen, both of these factors may contribute towards the development of the ovaries of an individual bee. According to Meidell (1934), when the queen is removed from a colony the bulk of the foraging population tend to stay in the nest, so that under these conditions also there might well be a relatively large number of bees in the nest and, in consequence, a higher and more stable temperature might be maintained.

So far we can conclude that lack of strenuous activity together with sufficient food, a relatively high temperature and the presence of other bees, are all factors which facilitate ovary development in worker bumblebees.

Butler (1954) has recently shown that the queen honeybee produces a substance which the worker honeybees of her colony obtain by licking her, and that this "queen substance" is passed directly from worker to worker in regurgitated food and enables all the bees to know that their queen is present. Among other things queen substance has the effect of preventing the ovaries of worker honeybees from developing.

In an attempt to discover whether queen bumblebees produce anything equivalent to this substance Free (1958a) captured a number of worker bumblebees whilst they were foraging and confined groups of them in cages, each with a queen of its own species. He kept other groups of similar size in cages without queens. All the cages were provided with ample food and were kept at 30°C. (86°F.). It was found that after one week there was no apparent difference in the degree of ovary development between the bees that were kept with queens and those kept without them, so it seems that when other conditions are favourable for ovary development the presence of a queen exerts little or no direct influence. It seems unlikely that anything similar to honeybee queen substance circulates amongst the members of a bumblebee colony. Nobody has ever reported seeing the workers licking the body of their queen, and the only method by which such a substance could be distributed would be if it somehow got into the food-storage cells in the nest, and it is difficult to see how this could happen.

The behaviour of the queen may, however, have a marked influence in preventing workers from laying eggs, and possibly also in suppressing their ovary development, particularly during the earlier stages of colony growth. The queen always builds the egg-cells, and is in no way directly aided in this task by the workers, and thus the growth of her colony is dependent on the activities of the queen herself (p. 15). Whilst her colony is small a queen is perhaps able to suppress the tendency of any of her workers to build egg-cells, or to lay eggs, by dominating rebel individuals in the way that has been described (p. 55), and one occasionally sees queens attack particular workers even in quite small colonies. As the colony becomes larger one may suppose that the queen's dominating and 'policing' activities are no longer effective in inhibiting all the workers from building egg-cells and laying eggs in them. The fact that the queen is becoming old may also be important in this connection. It may also be true that the scent of their queens is more apparent to the workers of small colonies.

Even in large colonies, however, the aggressive tendencies of the queen, and of a few dominant workers, probably keep the majority of the workers away from the egg-cells. Such behaviour may, therefore, contribute to the maintenance of colony stability, and to an effective division of labour.

Another extremely interesting, although largely unexplained, phenomenon which seems to be associated with the presence of laying workers may occur at about the time that males and queens are produced. Whilst the queen of a colony is laying her eggs some of the workers gather round and try to snatch the eggs from the cells and, if successful, rapidly proceed to eat them. The queen does her best to defend her newly laid eggs, sometimes continually revolving round her egg-cell in an effort to prevent the workers from approaching, and attacking the worst offenders.

Often, however, whilst she is engaged in pursuing one bee another dashes up to the cell and attempts to steal an egg. Having managed to lay a batch of eggs the queen quickly closes the cell and remains near it for the next few hours, repelling any bees who come too near. Her aggressive behaviour toward them reminds one of the dominant behaviour we have already discussed, although it should be pointed out that in none of the experiments on dominance were any of the workers seen to eat an egg, and even when a dominant bee was away from her egg-clump and other bees approached it they merely incubated the eggs.

The efforts of a queen to protect her eggs are not always successful, and in colonies containing very pugnacious workers it is probable that some of the eggs are eaten from nearly every batch. Sladen (1912) observed one particular *B. lapidarius* queen build and lay eggs in three cells, each of which was completely destroyed by her workers! The attempts of workers to open egg-cells and devour the eggs decreases after a few hours, and it appears from the literature that these rebel workers do not attempt to eat eggs after they have been laid for twenty-four hours or so.

This egg-eating habit is only found in a few species of bumble-bees. It has frequently been noted in *B. lapidarius* colonies, and also in colonies of *B. lucorum* and *B. terrestris* (See Free 1955a). These species are all pollen-storers and, as we have noted (Chapter 4, p. 32), the destruction of eggs in colonies of these species may help lower the larva/worker ratio and so act as a factor in the initiation of queen-production. Although the majority of more recent observations on bumblebees have probably been made on pocket-making species, egg eating by members of pocket-making species has only been observed in colonies of the American species *B. fervidius* (Plath 1934).

From time to time different theories have been advanced to account for this "race-suicidal" habit as Sladen called it. As long ago as 1802 Huber, the famous blind Swiss biologist, suggested that workers steal eggs in order to "drink the milky juice". He thought that nature had devised this habit of bumblebees in order to prevent them from becoming so numerous as to preclude other species of insects from obtaining sufficient nourishment.

Needless to say this idea was put forward long before Darwin had postulated the theory of Natural Selection! Many years later Pérez (1889) suggested that such egg-eating behaviour should be regarded as an imperfection of the social instinct which selection has not yet succeeded in correcting.

Sladen supposed that the egg-eating habit had arisen as a result of workers attempting to destroy eggs laid by invading *Psithyrus* queens (see Chapter 9, p. 71), and Lindhard (1912) who observed a *B. lapidarius* queen chew an egg that had been laid by a worker and "together with a little pollen, lay it on top of a cell of a queen larva", surmised, as a result of this isolated observation, that eggs laid by workers are used as food for queen larvae, and supposed that otherwise far too many male bees might be produced from the eggs laid by workers. Plath (1923a) was also originally inclined to accept this opinion. This hypothesis could easily be tested by observing the behaviour of workers who have recently eaten eggs to see whether or not they feed them to the larvae. But even if this does happen it does not explain why workers eat fertilised eggs laid by the queen.

We will not burden the reader with an hypothesis of our own since we are short of facts, not theories; and it is only by further investigation of this interesting behaviour that the correct explanation will be found.

CHAPTER 8

RECOGNITION OF FRIENDS AND FOES

*The dog that intends to bite growls; the bee
that intends to sting hums; but a girl only makes
her eyes sparkle.*

Polish Proverb

ANYBODY who has, accidentally or otherwise, disturbed a
bumblebees' nest will have discovered for himself that the
inhabitants will sometimes actively defend their home. Whereas
some species have the reputation of being relatively docile, others,
particularly some of those that habitually nest underground, can
be most ferocious and readily fly to attack an intruder. The
degree of hostility shown also depends on a colony's strength, the
aggressiveness of the individual bee apparently increasing with
the size of the colony.

The main weapon in a bumblebee's armoury is, of course,
her sting. The stings of worker and queen bumblebees, in
common with those of other social hymenoptera, have lost their
ancestral function as egg-laying instruments (ovipositors) and
have become modified as weapons of attack and defence. Once
the sting is thrust into the body of an adversary, poison, produced
from glands at its base, is injected through it. Some writers are
of the opinion that it is less painful to be stung by a bumblebee
than by a honeybee, but others definitely hold the opposite view,
so no doubt the amount of pain inflicted depends largely on the
sensitivity of the victim, or possibly on the species of the individual
bee.

The venom injected by bumblebees when they sting has not,
so far as we know, been analysed, but it seems improbable that
it is identical with that of honeybees, because people who are

relatively immune to honeybee venom often find that a single bumblebee sting produces a considerable swelling.

It is well known to beekeepers that the sting of the honeybee is barbed so that when it has entered human flesh she has great difficulty in withdrawing it again, and often in her efforts to do so the sting and surrounding tissues are torn from her body and left behind still attached to her enemy. However, the sting of a bumblebee has no barbs; consequently, bumblebees are always able to withdraw their stings from the bodies of their adversaries, but they can only sting effectively two or three times within a short period. This is probably because their supply of venom has been temporarily exhausted.

Bumblebees of all species, but especially the so-called carder bees, often assume a very characteristic attitude when their nests are disturbed. They roll half over onto their backs with the middle, and sometimes also the hind-legs, of one side raised, with their mandibles wide open and their stings protruding, all ready to attack the intruder. Bumblebees who have adopted these attitudes have been likened by Hudson (1892) to "a troupe of acrobats balancing themselves on their heads and hands, and kicking their legs about in the air". (Pl. 14a, p. 67).

Whilst she is in this position, or when she is picked up, a bumblebee will sometimes forcibly squirt out her rectal contents in a thin jet for a distance of several inches. Whether this behaviour be defensive or not is difficult to say, but it may perhaps have the effect of causing an intruder that has gripped a bumblebee to release its hold.

Plath (1934) observed that B. fervidius workers sometimes make use of an unique method of defence which, apparently, has not been observed to be employed by bees of any other species. If an intruder to a B. fervidius colony happens to be either comparatively weak, or else to possess no sting, it will often be seized and stung by the workers in the normal manner, but if, on the other hand, it possesses an equal or superior fighting ability to that of the B. fervidius workers themselves, they use a more subtle method of attack. Each defender cautiously approaches the intruder and daubs a drop of regurgitated honey onto its body. Very soon the intruder becomes so thoroughly wet and sticky that it retreats from the nest. The members of a B. fervidius colony will employ this method when dealing with intruding *Psithyrus* females and other bumblebees.

Bumblebees often need to defend themselves and their comb against the attacks of a wide variety of intruders. Some of these behave as robbers and try to carry off the food-stores of a colony; and weak colonies in nest-boxes are sometimes overwhelmed by invading worker honeybees or wasps who may completely rob them of their stores of honey, although the members of strong colonies will quickly and effectively deal with them.

Bumblebees themselves will also rob other colonies. Sometimes a robber bumblebee will enter the nest of another colony, fill her honey-stomach from the honeypots and then fly off, returning every few minutes to repeat the performance without the owners of the nest appearing to take the least notice of her. At other times the robber bumblebees will be seized by the occupants and dealt with very ferociously. To what extent bumblebees attempt to rob other colonies in nature is difficult to say, but several cases have been reported of bumblebees even attempting to enter honeybee colonies in search of food. Such bumblebees often meet with an untimely end; whilst examining honeybee colonies beekeepers sometimes find dead bumblebees, some of which have had all their hairs stripped off. Not only do bumblebees sometimes enter the nests of strange colonies in search of food, but it also appears to be quite common for bumblebee queens who are seeking nest-sites to enter, and try to establish themselves in, the nests of other bumblebees (see Chapter 9, p. 76).

The members of a bumblebee colony are certainly able to distinguish between members of their own colony and strangers from other colonies (Free 1958b), and it is interesting to observe the behaviour of bumblebees of different colonies towards one another. If one arranges an experiment so that some of the worker bumblebees of a colony stray into the nest of another colony of their own species, they are often attacked. Although under such circumstances the intruder may be stung to death, more often than not the owners of the nest merely grapple with her for a short time; eventually she manages to hide herself under the comb or in the nesting material, where she is left in comparative peace. The next day one finds such intruders apparently fully accepted as members of the colony whose nest they have inadvertently entered, and already taking an active part in its work. Sometimes, however, intruding bumblebees are completely ignored by the members of the recipient colony, and the intruders soon join in all its activities.

It is comparatively easy to strengthen colonies by introducing into the nests foragers of the same species who have been captured some miles away. If the bees introduced are caught nearer home, many of them are likely to return to their own nests when they have the chance. Strangers are best introduced at dusk, and the entrances to the nests to which they have been added should be closed afterwards, so that the bees introduced can become conditioned to their new home before they are allowed to fly on the following morning, by which time many of them will be found to have adopted the nest as their own.

If an intruding bumblebee belongs to another species the story is very different; and she is often killed. Even in such cases, however, the intruders are sometimes accepted and one may find bees of different *Bombus* species living peacefully together in the same nest. In one of his experiments Free removed a nest-box containing a colony of *B. lucorum* whilst some of its bees were out foraging, and put in its place a nest-box containing a *B. hortorum* colony. The next day the vestibule to the latter nest-box contained some dead workers of both species, but ten *B. lucorum* foragers were inside the nest itself, apparently living quite peacefully with the *B. hortorum* occupants. Experiments of this kind do not always produce such a result, however, and when another *B. hortorum* colony was put in the position formerly occupied by a *B. terrestris* colony all the inhabitants of the *B. hortorum* colony were killed by the more numerous *B. terrestris* foragers. Sladen, also, had great difficulty in getting bumblebees of different species to fraternise in the same nest, except when the colonies concerned were very small.

One of the methods often used by experimenters to stimulate a queen to lay eggs is to confine her in a nest-box with workers of some other species which nests earlier in the year (see p. 170); these workers will often continue to live peacefully with the bees that are produced from the queen's eggs. Probably the easiest method of inducing bumblebees of different species to live together in the same nest, is to place some cocoons of one species in the nest of the other, although even then some of the workers are likely to be attacked and killed when they emerge (Sladen 1912; Plath 1934).

We have said little, so far, about the behaviour of a bumblebee who finds herself in a strange nest. In such circumstances, she often appears very excited, and when examined by the inmates usually attempts to make good her escape; but occasionally such intruders have been observed to draw their wings and legs close to their bodies, telescoping the segments of their abdomens and remaining quite motionless (Sladen 1900; Frison 1928; and Free 1958b). Such behaviour appears to discourage would-be attackers. Bumblebees may also "sham dead" if they are suddenly gripped by a leg and whipped from the ground; but how such behaviour may assist their survival is obscure.

It has been known for some time that all the individuals in an ant or honeybee colony possess the same distinctive odour, and that they are able to distinguish members of other colonies by their strange odours. It was considered likely that bumblebees also recognise strangers by their odours, but the possibility that the behaviour of the strangers aroused suspicion, as sometimes happens in the case of honeybee intruders, could not be excluded without experiment. In order to determine whether bumblebee intruders can be recognised as such by their odour alone, Free carried out the following experiments. Workers from one colony were anaesthetized with nitrous oxide; while still unconscious they were placed on the comb of another colony, and the behaviour of the members of this colony towards them was closely studied. As a control, members of the recipient colony were also taken from their nest, anaesthetized, and then returned to it again. Whereas the colony's own bees were only examined

---

Plate 13 (opposite). THE END OF A COLONY
Once a colony has reared males and young queens it produces no more workers, and its population rapidly declines until the combs are deserted. Only the young, mated queens survive the winter to found new colonies the following year.
above.   An old B. pratorum queen rests on the ruins of her comb (x 1·6)
below.   Abandoned comb of B. lucorum colony. It has been destroyed by wax-moth larvae (x 1·6)

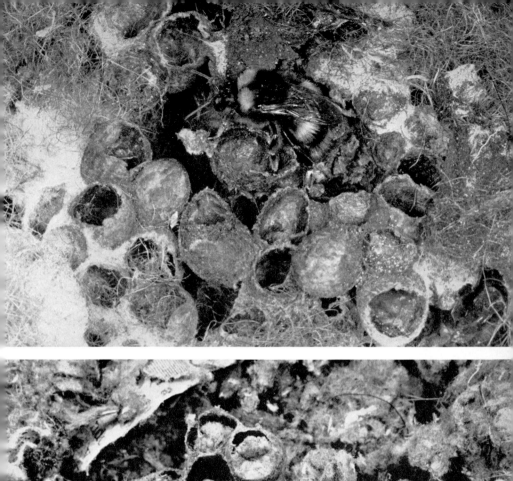

Plate 13

Plate 14

briefly and then ignored, many of the bees from the strange colony were attacked, often very vigorously. Since any effect of behaviour had been eliminated in these experiments, it is clear that bumblebees can recognise strangers by their odours alone.

An attempt was next made to try to find out how the members of a colony come to possess a similar odour. Workers were taken from a *B. agrorum* colony and kept for an hour or two in a nest containing the comb of another *B. agrorum* colony, but no bees. These experimental bees were then anaesthetized and returned to their own colony, whereupon many of them were attacked. Similar results were obtained when bees were merely suspended in wire-gauze cages over the combs of strange colonies and then returned to their own nests. It appears that these bees had acquired the alien odours of the strange colonies on their body surfaces, and that this had caused the hostility of their nest-mates when they were returned to them.

It is known that honeybees are capable of retaining odours in the wax which covers the surfaces of their bodies, and it seems likely that the surface of a bumblebee, which is covered with an abundance of hairs coated with wax (Schmidt 1939) will retain odours quite as readily. It is probable, as has been suggested in the case of honeybees, that the absorption, into the surface waxes of bumblebees, of the combined odours of their combs, food and nesting materials, contributes towards the acquisition of a common odour by all its members. One occasionally sees bumblebees who have just entered their own nests being attacked by their sisters, and it seems probable that these bees have somehow acquired an alien odour while away from their own colonies.

However, even if bees are suspended in a cage over a strange colony for a whole day, so that they can absorb its odours onto their bodies, they are often attacked if they are subsequently introduced into this strange colony; so it seems that the existence

---

Plate 14 (opposite). COLONY DEFENCE
Bumblebees have to defend themselves and their colonies against many enemies.
above.   *B. lucorum* worker lying on her back in a typical defensive attitude. She is ready to grasp and sting any intruder (x 1·0)
below.   A guard bee stationed just inside the entrance tunnel of a *B. lucorum* nest (x 2·5)

of a characteristic odour common to all the members of a colony cannot be fully explained by the absorption onto their bodies of the odour of their environment.

It has recently been postulated that the members of a honeybee colony acquire similar body odours as a result of its individual members sharing the same food. This hypothesis is quite feasable so far as honeybees are concerned, since honeybee workers of all ages frequently feed one another, so that widespread sharing of the nectar collected from the different kinds of flowers takes place. However, no direct transfer of food between adults normally occurs in bumblebee colonies, and it is unlikely that the individual bees of a colony take similar proportions of the kinds of nectar available in the honeypots. Furthermore, some of the foragers of a colony may be absent from their nest for much of the day, and they probably only feed on nectar from the particular species of flowers on which they are working. In our present state of knowledge it seems possible, therefore, that the distinctive odours of the bumblebees of different colonies are partly inherited.

We have seen how the members of a colony react more violently to strange bees belonging to another species than to strange bees of their own species. This most probably happens because of a greater difference in odour between bees of different species than between members of the same species. Sladen comments on the fact that the comb of each species of bumblebee has its own characteristic smell, and says that the smell of the bees resembles that of their combs. On one occasion he placed a small pellet of wax from a *B. ruderatus* comb into a *B. lapidarius* nest and found that it threw the occupants into an "uproar". The species odour is especially evident in the males and no doubt serves to attract queens to the mating stations established by males of their own species (see Chapter 5, p. 38).

In Chapter 6, p. 45, we saw that there is a division of labour among the members of a colony into house-bees and foragers. Some of the members of a colony will act much more readily in its defence than others; this is also true of honeybee colonies. Certain bumblebee workers actually become nest guards. Such guard bees have so far only been recorded in strong colonies of *B. lucorum* and *B. terrestris*, although they are probably present in large colonies of other species as well. This may partly explain why large colonies defend themselves more readily than smaller ones.

In naturally occurring *B. lucorum* and *B. terrestris* nests guards can sometimes be seen just inside the entrance tunnels and they are also often present in the entrance tunnels, and at the entrances to the nests, of colonies of these species when they are housed in nest-boxes. The guards stand facing away from the nest and, with their antennae, rapidly examine incoming bees. Only a small proportion of the bees of a colony ever undertake guard duty, but those that do so often act as guards for several days in succession. However, a guard rarely remains on duty for more than a few hours at a time, and most guards go foraging sometime during the day. Whilst on duty individual guards tend to be faithful to a particular part of the entrance tunnel, in much the same way as a honeybee will guard a particular part of her hive entrance, although they often patrol its entire length.

Whereas guard bumblebees readily attack honeybees or wasps who are placed in the entrance tunnels of their nests, they show a certain reluctance to come to grips with bumblebee intruders that are as powerful as themselves. Often a guard will rush up to a strange bumblebee who has been introduced into the tunnel, make threatening gestures, and then, instead of attacking her, will dash back again to the nest entrance where she will remain with her abdomen curved round towards the tunnel and her sting protruding.

In small colonies no guard-bees are apparent and it seems probable that guards are only mounted when their colonies have sufficient workers present to satisfy their essential nursing and foraging requirements. Although no guards are mounted in small colonies there are, nevertheless, usually certain particularly pugnacious workers, who are much more inclined to defend their colonies than are their sisters (Wagner 1907, Meidell 1934, Free 1958b). Such bees may attack nearly every intruder that enters their nest whereas other members of their colonies scarcely seem to realise that a stranger is present.

We have noted previously (p. 54) that the aggressiveness shown by the dominant member of a colony is associated in some way with the degree of development of her ovaries. After recording the hostility shown by individual bees of several small colonies towards intruders, Free dissected them and measured the degree of development of their ovaries. Once again it became apparent that their aggressiveness was linked with the development of their ovaries, as those of the more pugnacious workers were generally more developed.

In this chapter we have discussed the abilities of bumblebees to recognise enemies and friends, and have seen how they defend their colonies. In the next two chapters we will consider some of their more common enemies.

CHAPTER 9

CUCKOO BUMBLEBEES

And being fed by us you used us so
As that ungentle gull, the cuckoo's bird,
Useth the sparrow.
SHAKESPEARE. *Henry IV*

ALTHOUGH we shall devote a chapter to discussion of the predators and parasites of bumblebee colonies, the parasitic bumblebees, all of which belong to the genus *Psithyrus,* are so interesting that they deserve a chapter of their own.

Bumblebees of the genus *Psithyrus* so closely resemble those of the genus *Bombus,* whose habits we have discussed in earlier chapters, that bees of these two genera have often been confused. Nevertheless, there are some well-marked and interesting differences between them. For instance the outer covering (cuticle) of a *Psithyrus* is always much thicker and tougher than that of a *Bombus;* furthermore, the former possess longer stings, but have no pollen-baskets or similar structures in which to carry pollen. The name *Psithyrus* is derived from a Greek word meaning 'whispering' and probably alludes to the soft hum these bees make when flying.

The *Psithyrus* have no worker caste of their own and are dependent on other bumblebees for their propagation. The term 'queen' as applied by some authors to a *Psithyrus* female, is, therefore, somewhat misleading. As she has no pollen-baskets a *Psithyrus* female is quite unable to start a colony of her own; instead she enters the already established nest of a bumblebee colony and, if not killed or repulsed by its inhabitants, she lays eggs which the workers of this colony rear. In this way *Psithyrus* males and females are produced, and it is the similarity of habit of the female *Psithyrus* with that of the Cuckoo that has earned *Psithyrus* the title of 'cuckoo bumblebees'.

There are several different species of *Psithyrus*, each of which is parasitic on one or more different species of *Bombus*. The *Psithyrus* females usually emerge from their winter's rest a few weeks later than the *Bombus* species they parasitize and soon afterwards begin their search for *Bombus* nests.

It seems that it is the scent of a bumblebee colony that enables a *Psithyrus* female to find it, and it is probable that the females of each *Psithyrus* species instinctively search for the characteristic species odour of their hosts. In those cases in which two or more *Bombus* species are parasitized by one and the same *Psithyrus* species, it would be interesting to try to discover whether the two *Bombus* species concerned have somewhat similar odours. Sladen (1912) noted that most of the nests in which he found *Psithyrus* invaders had comparatively short entrance tunnels, and this led him to suggest that colonies with long entrance tunnels may be more successful in avoiding parasitization by *Psithyrus* females. However, Plath (1934) has found *Psithyrus* females in nests with entrance tunnels up to ten feet long, so it seems doubtful whether long entrance tunnels really do afford much protection. Little is known about the behaviour of *Psithyrus* females when they are searching for nests; it would be interesting to discover whether they normally search in the sort of place where nests of their host species are particularly likely to occur.

Apparently *Psithyrus* females sometimes enter the nests of species other than those of their own particular host, and use them as temporary lodgings until they succeed in finding a colony of the right species. *Psithyrus* females may even try to enter honeybee colonies in search of a temporary abode or, more likely, food. Plath (1927) has given us a vivid description of a *Psithyrus* queen being forcibly ejected from a beehive with a mass of worker honeybees clinging to her.

The reception that a *Psithyrus* intruder receives when she first enters a *Bombus* nest seems to depend on several factors, the most important of which appear to be the size and kind of colony which she is invading, and also her own behaviour.

Sometimes for the first few hours she will try to avoid all contact with the *Bombus* queen and workers, and hides herself under the comb and nesting material, and only gradually ingratiates herself with the inhabitants. Frison (1926a), when describing the parasitization of *Bombus americanorum* by *Psithyrus variabilis*, suggested that one of the secrets of a successful invasion of a nest was the calm and deliberate behaviour of the *Psithyrus* female. If she was molested by the workers whose nest she had entered, she drew her legs up close against her body and remained quite motionless for some time, behaviour of a kind which we have also seen to occur when *Bombus* workers are introduced into strange colonies (Chapter 8, p. 66). Somewhat similar be-haviour has also been recorded among other animals, such as honeybees, birds and wolves.

In direct contrast to this sort of behaviour some observers have recorded how *Psithyrus* females immediately attacked the *Bombus* workers and grabbed many of them as though to sting them, but usually quickly released them again. After a short while such aggressive behaviour steadily declined until once again peace reigned in the colonies.

The *Bombus* workers themselves may remain far from passive and, especially in populous colonies, a *Psithyrus* female will some-times be seized by several workers who form a 'ball' round her and try to sting her, in much the same way as honeybee workers sometimes attack a queen honeybee who has recently been introduced to their colony. Some of the *Bombus* workers on the outside of such a 'ball' may inadvertently sting and kill some of their fellows in their attempts to sting the intruder. It seems that when a colony contains egg-laying workers a *Psithyrus* female has great difficulty in getting herself accepted; from what we know of the aggressive tendencies of laying workers (Chapter 7, p. 53) this is exactly what one would expect.

Bombus workers find it very difficult to kill a *Psithyrus* female because of her many defensive characteristics. We have already mentioned that the body of a *Psithyrus* female is covered with thicker 'armour' than that of a *Bombus* queen or worker, and the membranous hinges between the segments of the abdomen of a *Psithyrus* are toughened and not so soft. Her anus and the connecting tissues between head and thorax, which is probably her most vulnerable part, and between thorax and abdomen, are also well protected. She also possesses offensive characters—

a more powerful sting, and more pointed jaws with stronger muscles.

It is small wonder that even when a *Psithyrus* female has been killed by the inhabitants of a colony, it is often only after she has inflicted a heavy toll of casualties. Plath saw a *P. laboriousus* female enter a *B. terricola* colony and in the ensuring battle both she and fifteen *B. terricola* workers were killed.

In his experience Sladen found that in colonies of *B. lapidarius* and *B. terrestris* which were parasitized by *P. rupestris* and *P. vestalis* respectively, the *Psithyrus* intruder invariably eventually killed the *Bombus* queen, and he suggested that this is always the case. However, observation on other species of *Psithyrus* has shown that the *Bombus* queen and the *Psithyrus* intruder do sometimes live in peace together, even until the colony eventually dies out. Plath had one colony under observation in which the *B. affinis* queen and *P. ashtoni* invader lived together for two months without showing any hostility towards each other, and he suggested that "further inquiry into the queen-killing habit of *Psithyrus rupestris* and *P. vestalis* will undoubtedly show that Sladen based his conclusion on insufficient evidence". However, it seems probable that this discrepancy may be explained by differences in the ferocity of the species concerned.

Sladen supposed that a duel between a *Bombus* queen and *Psithyrus* intruder of the species which he studied, was often started by the *Bombus* queen, as a result of her jealousy of the *Psithyrus* female, about the time that the latter was ready to lay eggs. This theory seems quite plausible, since we know that queens or dominant *Bombus* workers are most aggressive to the members of their colonies who have developed ovaries, and also that two *Bombus* queens often do not tolerate each other's presence when both have well developed ovaries.

If a *Psithyrus* is to succeed in her task of propagating her own kind, it seems important that the colony she invades should not be so small that there are insufficient workers to rear her brood nor, on the other hand, so populous that the workers succeed in destroying her. Both Hoffer (1889) and Sladen were of the opinion that *Psithyrus* females usually invade those colonies of their host species which have moderate numbers of workers. Undoubtedly the time when *Psithyrus* females emerge from hibernation helps the attainment of this end. According to Sladen a *Psithyrus* female will delay the killing of her host-queen if the colony she finds herself in is too small.

One of the most striking things about the parasitization by *Psithyrus* females is that even when a *Psithyrus* and a *Bombus* queen live together amicably and both lay eggs, very few, if any, adults are ever produced from the *Bombus* eggs. The same thing happens when the *Bombus* workers of an invaded colony lay eggs. From the observations of Sladen it seems likely that the *Psithyrus* females eat any *Bombus* eggs that are laid, and Plath has recorded seeing a *Psithyrus* female even destroy a small clump of *Bombus* larvae.

Bombus females nearly always possess eight ovarioles—four in each of their ovaries. In *Psithyrus* females, however, the number may be much greater and is by no means constant. Cumber (1949b) found that it varied from six to as many as eighteen per ovary. In association with this one would expect a *Psithyrus* female to have a relatively high egg-laying potential, and Sladen once saw a *Psithyrus* female lay twenty-three eggs in six minutes!

So far as we know the *Psithyrus* larvae are looked after entirely by the workers of their host colonies. A *Psithyrus* female apparently neither feeds nor incubates her own brood; indeed, the relative inflexibility of her abdomen is not suited to incubation. The number of male and female *Psithyrus* produced in a colony obviously depends to a large extent on the size of the worker population of the host colony. Plath recorded the production of more than eighty *P. ashtoni* males and females in a populous colony of *B. affinis*. Again, there often is a great variation in the size of the *Psithyrus* females produced; some of them may be no larger than *Bombus* workers of average size. However, the behaviour of such small *Psithyrus* females seems to be quite typical of their kind, and not to differ from that of the larger ones. Like them they remain in their host colony for as long as possible, and soon after they have left it seek places in which to hibernate.

We must now consider the interesting question of the probable origin of these parasitic bumblebees. It is generally agreed that the bees of the genus *Psithyrus* have evolved in some way from those of the genus *Bombus*. However, all the species of *Psithyrus* could have been descended from a single common ancestral group (monophyletic descent) or, again, some of them could have had separate evolutionary histories (polyphyletic descent).

Richards (1927c) discusses these two possibilities and shows that there is much to be said for both viewpoints. He listed twenty-seven morphological characters possessed by *Psithyrus* but not by *Bombus*. Although he classified as many as possible of these as adaptations to a parasitic mode of life, so that they might, therefore, reasonably be considered to result from convergent evolution, he was still left with eight characters which cannot be accounted for in this way. Hence it may be argued that the genus *Psithyrus* is of monophyletic descent, since there are greater resemblances between bees of the various species of *Psithyrus* than there are between any particular species of *Psithyrus* and its *Bombus* host. However, as Richards pointed out, the different species of *Psithyrus* are quite distinct from each other and, despite the fact that they do not resemble their hosts, they can still be regarded as having had a polyphyletic descent.

Turning aside from morphological evidence for the moment, let us consider how this parasitism may have arisen. Sladen found that various species of *Bombus* showed parasitical tendencies. He discovered that queens of the species *B. terrestris* and *B. lapidarius* occasionally do not trouble to start colonies for themselves but attempt to take over colonies already founded by other queens of the same species. In such cases the foundress and intruder queens fight for possession of the nest and one or other is killed. Sometimes several such duels may be fought for a single nest, and in one particular nest Sladen discovered the bodies of no less than twenty *B. terrestris* queens!

Sladen not only found that *B. terrestris* queens enter nests belonging to other *B. terrestris* queens, but that they also sometimes occupy nests of the closely related species *B. lucorum*. When a *B. terrestris* invader succeeded in killing a *B. lucorum* queen, he found that the *B. lucorum* workers present helped to rear the future *B. terrestris* brood in the same way as they would have reared the brood of a *Psithyrus* female. According to Lindhard (1912) *B. distinguendus* queens will also parasitize *B. subterraneous* colonies, and Plath records that queens of *B. affinis* will invade and parasitize the colonies of *B. terricola* queens.

It is easy to imagine how a more permanent parasitism of one species on another could arise in this way. Richards points out that a bumblebee queen nearly always 'parasitizes' colonies of her own or of a closely related species, and that this habit would lead to a polyphyletic origin of bees of the genus *Psithyrus*, "each species being restricted to one or to a few related species".

In each of the cases, recorded above, of queen *Bombus* of one species being parasitic upon another species, the parasitic species emerges later in the spring than does her host, so that the parasitism may have arisen as a result of queens of the later emerging species stumbling upon colonies of their host species whilst searching for nest-sites. Richards postulated that species of the genus *Psithyrus* tend to have been derived from southern *Bombus* species at the northern edge of their geographical range, and he supposed that queens of such species emerge from hibernation at temperatures which are governed by their southern origin and so appear later in the spring than the species better adapted to the local climate. In such circumstances the conditions appropriate for the development of parasitism are present. In support of this view he mentioned that *B. terrestris* which, as we have seen, is occasionally parasitic on *B. lucorum,* in general has a more southerly distribution than the latter. He also noted that the *Psithyrus* species generally tend to have the colouration and shorter hairs characteristic of more southerly races of bumblebees.

Reinig (1935) studied the geographical distribution of individual bumblebee species and their particular parasitic *Psithyrus* species. Although he found that their distribution may coincide completely in the case of one or two pairs of species, more generally the distribution of the parasite does not extend to the same limits as those of her host. In this connection he mentions that *Psithyrus* species are scarce at high altitudes and do not appear to be present in Greenland, although *Bombus* species have been recorded from there. These findings seem to provide further support for Richard's view.

Reinig also compiled a list of *Psithyrus* species together with their *Bombus* hosts, and came to the conclusion that, although there are some startling exceptions, the cuckoo bee in most cases strongly resembles her principal host. Thus *Psithyrus vestalis* resembles her host *B. terrestris* in colour and markings, and *Psithyrus distinctus* resembles her host *B. lucorum*. Richards had been less definite about this resemblance between parasite and host and wrote "although the details of the colour-pattern of host and parasite do not resemble one another in a significant way, yet these patterns appear to be governed in part by the same fundamental laws".

In order to account for this similarity in colour-pattern Reinig put forward the theory that a *Psithyrus* species and her host species were originally descended from the same common stock, and hence had a similar genetic constitution. He argued that since both host and parasite live under the same ecological, geographical and climatic conditions, the genetic constitution they have in common is likely to have been influenced in the same direction, and hence they have often attained similar colouration. He supposed that their evolution was also influenced in a similar way by the fact that both parasite and host live under conditions which may be specific to the nests of the host species.

In proposing this theory Reinig was influenced by the fact that he could not see any advantage that a *Psithyrus* species would gain from resembling her host species and did not, therefore, see how such similarity could have come about by Natural Selection. It is certainly true that, once inside the nest of her host, the colouration of a *Psithyrus* female is of no value in helping her to ingratiate herself with the inhabitants, but as Hoffer has seen the guards of a colony attack and chase away a *Psithyrus* female who was attempting to enter their nest, it is possible that the possession of a similar colouration to her host may be of advantage to a *Psithyrus* female attempting to enter a nest. It is also probable that, since *Psithyrus* species appear to occupy the same geographical areas as their host species, their resemblance to the more numerous host species is of some advantage in protecting them from predators.

We may summarise by saying that although morphological evidence seems, on the whole, to indicate that all the *Psithyrus* species are descended from a common ancestor, other evidence seems to suggest that parasitism has developed within closely related species, so that species of *Psithyrus* as a whole have two or more lines of descent. This common relationship of a parasite to her host would also account for such similarities in colour as occur between them, although this similarity may have been enhanced by selection enabling the parasite to escape its enemies.

There is another point that is worth considering. We know (p. 66) that colonies have their own individual odours, and that the differences in odour between colonies belonging to different species seem to be greater than that between colonies of the same species. It is perhaps relevant in this connection that when a bumblebee queen invades a colony of a strange species this species is always a closely related one. Presumably one of the factors which helps her to establish herself is that the odours of closely related species are similar. It may well be that *Psithyrus* females possess odours similar to those of their host species, and one would suppose that it is much more important for a *Psithyrus* female to resemble her host species in smell than in colouration. The odour common to the members of a colony may partly result from individuals absorbing on their bodies the combined odours of nesting material and comb. It is perhaps significant that when a *Psithyrus* female first enters a nest she often hides under the comb or nesting material for some time, for by so doing she may, in fact, be acquiring an odour similar to that of the colony's inhabitants.

CHAPTER 10

ENEMIES OF BUMBLEBEES

The honey bags steal from the humble-bees,
And, for night-tapers, crop their waxen thighs

SHAKESPEARE. *A Midsummer Night's Dream*

BUMBLEBEES are directly dependent upon plants for food and for the raw materials for constructing their combs, as well as for nest-material. Their dependence on other animal species is limited to occupying the disused nests of mammals or birds. On the other hand many animals rely directly or indirectly upon bumblebees for their livelihood, and the bumblebees provide a link between them and the plant life upon which all animal life ultimately depends.

Bumblebees are attacked, both in their immature and adult stages, by predators and parasites of various kinds. Other animals feed on the food stored in their combs and even on the combs themselves, and many others act as scavengers and feed on the waste substances of the bumblebee colonies. Still other species found in a bumblebees' nest often have no particular business there at all, and are simply using it as a temporary abode.

Long lists of species of animals have been recorded living in bumblebees' nests. Many of these are insects belonging to the Coleoptera (beetles), Diptera (two-winged flies) and Lepidoptera (butterflies and moths). The Rev. Tuck (1896 and 1897) records over sixty species of beetles alone. In this chapter we shall only describe the more important and interesting species. For additional information the reader is referred to Sladen (1912), Frison (1926a), Plath (1934) and Cumber (1949b).

Bumblebees are not specifically preyed upon by any particular type of predator, but probably form welcome additions to the diet of quite a few. Bumblebee combs are readily eaten by many kinds of small mammals, and Darwin (1859) quotes Col. Newman (p. 140) as estimating that two-thirds of the bumblebee colonies in England are destroyed by field-mice. Sladen and Plath also stated that mice often destroy colonies, especially those in their incipient stages which are often left unguarded for long periods whilst their queens are out foraging. Badgers can be serious enemies of the bumblebee; of 80 colonies of *B. agrorum* observed by Cumber as many as 17 were destroyed by badgers and by rodents of various kinds.

In America, skunks are also a menace to bumblebees. In order to see how a skunk manages to deal with a bumblebee colony, Plath gave a captive specimen a large bumblebee nest containing about 75 workers. "The first thing the skunk did was to scratch at the nest. This was immediately answered by a shrill chorus from within. As the workers came rushing out, they were seized one by one with the front paws and rolled on the ground for a few seconds with a quick, alternating, back-and-forth movement of both paws, and then eaten with a crunching noise." After three-quarters of an hour all the bees had been eaten and the comb as well!

Birds seem generally to avoid bumblebees, as they do other insects with vivid warning or aposematic colouration (Carrick 1936); but bumblebees, in common with most insects, have been recorded as the prey of many different birds from time to time. They are probably particularly vulnerable when lethargic while spending the night away from their nests or during hibernation. Bumblebees are also prone to become drowsy whilst foraging on certain flowers such as those of the lime and rhododendron whose nectar in a concentrated form is mildly toxic, and cases of birds preying on them under such circumstances are on record.

The greatest enemies of bumblebees among the birds are probably the shrikes, of which our own red-backed shrike (*Lanius collurio*) is a typical example. The beaks of these birds, being notched and hooked at the tip, are beautifully adapted for seizing animal prey of which large insects form a major part, and they often impale their victims on thorns.

Probably the only insect predators which attack bumblebees

on the wing are the robber-flies (*Asilidae*), many of which are large and powerful. A robber-fly seizes and holds its prey in its strong legs and, having inserted its proboscis into its victim's body, proceeds to suck up its blood. The largest robber-fly in this country, *Asilus crabroniformis*, is known to prey on honeybees, solitary bees and wasps, and although bumblebees have not apparently been recorded among its victims there can be little doubt that they are sometimes included. In America, Plath regards the robber-flies as important enemies of bumblebees, and has observed *Dasyllis grossa* capturing bumblebees and feeding on them. The large robber-fly of New Zealand (*Asilus varius*) has also be seen to attack bumblebees (Smith—quoted by Thomson 1922).

An important internal parasite of queen bumblebees and *Psithyrus* females is the nematode worm *Sphaerularia bombi* which is found both in Europe and in America. The first account of its life-history was given by Leuckart (1885 a, b), and, later workers have made important additions to our knowledge of it (see Stein 1956a).

During the summer the nematode is free-living in moist soil, where copulation between the males and females takes place. In late summer or autumn the fertilised female nematodes enter the abdomens of queens which have burrowed themselves into the soil to hibernate. Palm (1948) thinks they may gain entry into a bumblebee queen through her mouth, anus or genital opening, but Cumber is of the opinion that they burrow through the intersegmental membranes of the abdomen. Having entered a queen bumblebee the parasite apparently undergoes little further development during the winter whilst the queen is hibernating, but towards the end of hibernation the worm's genital organs develop into a large sac whilst its body degenerates into a tiny appendage. When fully developed the genital protuberance is about 1 cm. long—it has been estimated at about 20,000 times the size of the original worm—and contains several thousand eggs. Presently its walls rupture and the eggs escape to float freely in their host's abdominal cavity. They hatch soon afterwards, and the young worms wander about freely inside their host's body, often penetrating into various organs. When one realises that some queens are originally infected by a great

Plate 15.—Some Enemies of Bumblebees. Marking a Bumblebee
above. Enemies of Bumblebees. 1 *Conops vesicularis;* 2 *Fannia canicularis;*
3 *Asilus crabroniformis;* 4 *Brachycoma devia;* 5 *Volucella bombylans;* 6 *Asilus varius* (x 1.3).
below. Marking a bee under an anaesthetic (x 1.2).

Plate 16

many worms (Cumber recorded as many as sixty-eight in one queen) one gets some idea of the enormous number of these nematodes that can be produced in the body of a single queen bumblebee.

When a queen is infected with these nematode worms her ovaries fail to develop. Such queens can be seen on the wing a long time after they would normally have established colonies, their slower and more clumsy flight readily distinguishing them from unparasitized individuals. It has been suggested that infected queens, being unable to found colonies, return to their old or similar hibernating sites where, before they die, the young nematodes leave their bodies and become free once more. Since, as we have seen (Chapter 5, p. 42), the hibernating sites of queens are often of a specialised nature the nematodes are thus favourably placed to invade the bodies of further queens when they are hibernating during the following autumn and winter.

Often many queens found in spring are infected with this nematode. Cumber found that some species are more likely to be attacked than those of others; out of a total of 146 *B. lucorum* queens which he dissected one spring, 100 were parasitized. It is undoubtedly true that in certain areas the parasitization of queens by *Sphaerularia* is the most important single factor in reducing the number of bumblebee colonies and hence of the total bumblebee population.

Whereas *Sphaerularia* always parasitizes queen bumblebees, the larvae of certain Conopid flies are parasitic on worker bumblebees. The adult female flies are found in early June on or near flowers, where they lie in wait for foraging bumblebees. When a bumblebee comes along the waiting fly pounces on her and, clasping her momentarily in mid-air, thrusts her ovipositor through one of her intersegmental membranes and inserts an egg into her abdomen. The larva which hatches from this egg soon attaches itself to an air-sac within the body of its host. The presence of the larva is not immediately fatal, and it is not until

---

Plate 16 (opposite). ENTRANCES TO BUMBLEBEES' NESTS
above. B. *lucorum* forager leaving the entrance tunnel of a nest-box (x 2·5)
below. B. *pratorum* pollen-gatherer entering her nest under the floor of a barn (x 2·5)

the larva is quite large that the infected forager dies, whereupon the parasite consumes the remaining tissues of its host and then changes into a pupa whilst still sheltering inside the empty husk of the bee's abdomen. Here the pupa remains until early the following summer when the adult fly emerges and forces its way out. Conopid flies have been known to emerge from the abdomens of bumblebees which had been captured and pinned in a collection a year previously!

Workers infected with Conopid larvae often die inside their nest, when, as usually happens to dead workers, they are carried out of the entrance or pushed into some out of the way part of the nest by their sisters. When a colony has died out one can easily recognise such infected workers, because the presence of the parasites in their abdomens prevents them from shrinking in the usual way.

Cumber dissected nearly two hundred foraging workers and found that twelve per cent contained Conopid larvae, so this parasite may substantially reduce the bumblebee population in some districts. However, it must be remembered that workers can carry on foraging for some time after becoming infected, so perhaps the parasite does not have so serious an influence on bumblebee numbers as might at first be supposed.

Another interesting internal parasite is a tiny mite, probably a species of *Tarsonoemus*, which lives in the abdominal air-sacs of bumblebees. It was first described by Cumber, who gives the following account of its life history. The mites pass the winter in the bodies of hibernating queens. A few weeks after an infected queen emerges from hibernation, the mites lay eggs which hatch at about the time that the first worker bumblebees emerge in the colony she has founded. The method of infecting new individuals seems to be similar to that practised by the mite *Acarapis woodi*, which parasitizes honeybees. After mating, the young female mites move out through the abdominal spiracles and onto the body surfaces of the queens whence they transfer themselves onto the bodies of other bees, eventually gaining access to their air-sacs by way of the abdominal spiracles. Once inside its new host a mite pushes its proboscis through the wall of an air-sac and feeds on its host's body-juices. Presently this new generation of mites in its turn produces young; the whole cycle is then repeated and new worker bees become infected. Any bumblebee queens which emerge in the colony also ultimately become infected, and in this way the parasite is carried into hibernation inside the bodies of the young queens. Although a high proportion of the population of a colony may be infected, the mites do not seem to interfere with the activities of their hosts to any noticeable extent.

Bumblebees also sometimes become infected with a protozoan parasite, *Nosema bombi*. Like its close relation *Nosema apis*, which infects honeybees, this single-celled parasite often occurs in great numbers in the cells of the walls of the alimentary canal and of the malphigian tubules. Little is known about *Nosema bombi*. Fantham and Porter (1914) found it in several bumblebee species, particularly in *B. agrorum*; and Betts (1920a) found that the *B. agrorum* queens which she captured in spring were all infected with it. Infected bumblebees frequently lose the power of flight and crawl about in a blundering manner; eventually most of them die. Fantham and Porter have claimed that bumblebees can become infected with the species of *Nosema* (*N. apis*) which attacks honeybees and that *N. bombi* will also attack honeybees; they postulated that the robbing of honeybees' colonies by bumblebees, and vice versa, has resulted in interchange of these parasites. Although *Nosema bombi* can cause a heavy mortality among bumblebees one would suppose that queens are less seriously affected than workers, otherwise it is difficult to see how the parasite could survive the winter to infect new bumblebee colonies during the following spring. The whole question of the relationship between *Nosema bombi* and bumblebees is clearly in need of further investigation.

Apart from these parasites which attack adult bumblebees, there are others which attack their brood. Amongst the most important are the larvae of two species of Tachinid flies, *Brachycoma devia* (Pl. 15, p. 82) and *Brachycoma sarcophagina*, which parasitize bumblebee larvae in Europe and America respectively.

The adult flies make their appearance in late spring and begin to search for bumblebees' nests. Once inside a nest, they do not lay eggs but, instead, produce their young alive as tiny maggots. Similar 'viviparous' habits are found in scattered instances among many insect groups and are the result of the eggs being retained in the body of their mother until the larvae have hatched from them. The Tachinid larvae are typical maggots, translucent white in colour, tapering towards the head and bluntly rounded at the hind end, and are deposited in cells containing bumblebee eggs; possibly they may also be laid among bumblebee larvae.

While the bumblebee larvae are growing the Tachinid larvae accompanying them do not increase in size. But, as soon as the bumblebee larvae cease to feed, and spin their cocoons, the Tachinid larvae enter their bodies and proceed to devour them. In other words they wait until the bee larvae provide them with the biggest meals possible.

The usual number of Tachinid larvae in a parasitized cocoon varies from 1 to 4 but as many as 24 have been found (Cumber 1949b). Parasitized cocoons can usually be recognised by their soft watery appearance and, in heavily parasitized colonies, a characteristic, disagreeable odour permeates the whole nest. The larvae grow rapidly and may reach a length of ⅝ in. (16 mm.). When they have finished feeding they force their way out of the softened walls of the cocoons, leaving small regular holes, and rapidly migrate down into the bottom of the comb, or into the nest-material, where they pupate. After they have left the body of a larva upon which they have been feeding, it promptly collapses like an empty balloon.

The pupal stage may only last for 7 to 14 days before the adult flies appear. Several generations of this parasite may, therefore, be produced in a single season. Larvae produced late in the season do not pupate in the nest-material but migrate into the surrounding soil before doing so. They remain as pupae throughout the winter.

Tachinid larvae may take a heavy toll of bumblebee lives, and Plath reports finding a considerable number of colonies that had been completely destroyed by them. Cumber found that most colonies in England are infected by this parasite in some degree, and that colonies whose nests have exposed entrances are particularly liable to be heavily attacked.

The combs of bumblebee colonies, like those of honeybees, are often subject to the ravages of wax-moth larvae. The larvae of the bumblebee wax-moth which occurs in Europe, *Aphomia sociella*, will quickly ruin a comb by burrowing in it and eating the wax; according to both Hoffer (1882-83) and Sladen they sometimes eat the larvae and pupae as well. The larvae of this wax-moth, when fully grown, are about 1 in. to 1¼ in. (23-32 mm.) long. They spin large quantities of silk which, together with fragments of comb, they weave into tunnels, from which they sally forth to attack the comb only to dart back into cover again with amazing agility when molested by its owners. A heavily infected colony may contain as many as a hundred caterpillars and its comb can become completely dilapidated within a few days, nothing being left but a labyrinth of silken tunnels.

Bumblebees seem powerless to defend their comb against infestation by wax-moth larvae, and at the end of the season one often comes across colonies whose combs are riddled with them: the survivors remain helplessly on top of what little is left of their comb. Colonies in nest-boxes often come to an end in this way (Pl. 13b, p. 66): perhaps the adult moths can gain access to their combs more easily than to those of naturally situated colonies.

The American species of bumblebee wax-moth, *Vitula edmandsii*, is a smaller and comparatively harmless species, and is most often found in colonies which are on the decline. Its larvae feed on refuse, old comb and pollen but, unlike the larvae of the European bumblebee wax-moth, there is no evidence that they eat bumblebee brood. They pupate and hibernate in the tunnels where they lived as larvae, whereas the European bumblebee wax-moth larvae, when fully grown, move out of the comb and spin their cocoons close together, so that a solid mass of them is formed. Both species change to pupae in May and the adult moths emerge in June.

Let us now consider a few of the more common animals to be found living in a bumblebees' nest, which do not necessarily do the colony any harm, and in some cases may even perform services that are beneficial to the bees.

Every observer of bumblebees will be familiar with the small brown mites of the genus *Parasitus* which are to be found in a high proportion of the nests of every species. They were first described by Oudemans in 1902 who found them in a nest of *B. terrestris* and named them *Parasitus bomborum*. Probably, however, there are several species of these mites. They roam over the queens, workers, males and comb and sometimes are even found in the larval cells. Their food is not definitely known and so it is uncertain whether their presence is beneficial or harmful to a colony. Perhaps they feed on tiny scraps of pollen and other debris and serve a useful purpose in keeping the comb and bodies of the bees clean, but it is equally possible that they may also steal the food-stores of a colony.

It seems that the mites which survive the winter are those that attach themselves to young queens and are carried into hibernation with them. In the spring one frequently sees a queen that is foraging, or searching for a nest-site, with seething masses of mites clinging to her thorax and abdomen. They are thus already at hand to invade any new colonies which the queens may found.

In many nests larvae of Hoverflies of the genus *Volucella* are found. The adult flies are especially interesting because their colour-patterns resemble those of certain species of bumblebees. Their mimicry of their various bumblebee hosts does not stop at colour, however; their flight is similar to a bumblebee's and they can be readily mistaken for one on the wing, and, if they are disturbed when they have alighted, they even raise their middle legs and buzz in the same manner as bumblebees. The way in which these defenceless flies mimic their bumblebee hosts, whom many predators learn to leave alone, presumably helps to protect them. Whether or not these resemblances also help them to gain entry to a bumblebee colony is more doubtful.

Sladen found that when he killed a female *Volucella* she at once started to lay eggs, and he made the interesting suggestion that even if such gravid females are killed by the bumblebees whose colonies they have entered, they will nevertheless lay eggs and so play their part in propagating their species. *Volucella* eggs are coated with a sticky substance which immediately hardens in contact with the air, and it is probable that it not only fastens the eggs on to the material upon which they have been laid, but also helps to protect them from the bumblebees.

The bodies of *Volucella* larvae are broad and flat, tapering anteriorly. Some grow to about an inch (26 mm.) in length. Along the sides of their bodies there are two rows of small spines, and larger spines are arranged in a semi-circle around their posterior ends. They are mostly found beneath the combs, and they probably feed on any debris which accumulates at the bottom of their nests, such as bits of comb, wax, pollen and faeces. Only when their host colonies have almost died out do they invade the combs themselves.

The larvae of *Fannia*, another fly, are also found in bumblebee nests. The presence of prominent spines down the sides of their bodies, instead of only round the anus, as in the *Volucella* larvae, readily distinguishes them from the latter. The larvae of *Volucella* and of *Fannia* are particularly common in surface nests, and they undoubtedly serve a useful function as scavengers.

Small beetles belonging to the genus *Antherophagus* also live in bumblebees' nests, both as adults and as larvae. Not only do bumblebees provide these beetles with shelter and food but they also, albeit unwillingly, transport them to their nests in the first place! The adult beetles appear on flowers, in May, where they wait for a foraging bumblebee to come along. When a bumblebee visits the flower where one of these beetles is lurking the latter seizes the tongue, or an antenna, or leg of the bumblebee with its mandibles. Despite her efforts to get rid of her passenger, the bumblebee is apparently unable to do so and eventually carries it back to her nest where the beetle releases its hold and drops onto the comb. For a more detailed account of this unusual method of transport the reader is referred to the recent review by Frisch (1952). Once inside the nest the beetles make their way to the bottom of the comb where mating takes place and eggs are laid.

It was originally thought (Wagner 1907) that the larvae of *Antherophagus* could cause great destruction in bumblebees' nests but later observers suggest that they simply feed on refuse.

According to Scott (1920) and Frison (1921) the larvae pupate either in the comb, or, more probably, in the surrounding soil, and give rise to a second generation of adults which are to be found on flowers during July and August. These infest other nests and give rise to a further generation which hibernate as larvae, changing to pupae in the early summer of the following year.

In this chapter we have only considered the more common

and interesting predators, parasites and scavengers of bumblebees'
nests. The list of scavengers and occasional lodgers that have
been recorded in them is already formidable, and no doubt will
be greatly augmented in the future. One is indeed inclined to
marvel that bumblebees manage to continue to survive at all.
The various insects and other animals which are guests in the
nests of bumblebees form an interesting study on their own and,
when one considers that many of these guests are themselves
preyed upon and parasitized in their turn by other insects, one
realises that this study could occupy an observer for a life-time.

CHAPTER II

THE COLLECTION OF FOOD

The careful insect midst his works I view,
Now from the flowers exhaust the fragrant dew,
With golden treasures load his little thighs,
And steer his distant journey through the skies.

JOHN GAY. *Rural Sports*

THE essential foods—the raw materials—for the maintenance and growth of a bumblebee colony are nectar and pollen, and it is the task of its foraging force to collect them from the flowers of the surrounding countryside. Certain species, notably *B. lucorum* and *B. terrestris,* occasionally also collect honeydew, a sugary substance which is excreted by Aphids, and some other plant-sucking insects, on the leaves of plants (Hulkkonen 1929; Brian 1957). Although Fantham and Porter (1914) have mentioned that bumblebees collect water, their observation does not appear to have been confirmed by others (Pl. 18,p. 99).

The mouth-parts of a bumblebee can be extended from their folded, resting position beneath the head and collectively form a tube through which nectar is sucked from flowers and passes into the honey-stomach or crop, where it is stored until the forager arrives home. Female bumblebees (except in the genus *Psithyrus*) have special structures, the paired corbiculae or pollen-baskets, one on each of their hind-legs, into which they pack the pollen as it is collected and carry it back to their nests (Pl. 18, p. 99).

The amount of nectar collected by a foraging bumblebee depends very much on the weather conditions at the time, as well as on the kind of flower which she visits, and it is evident that foragers do not necessarily fill their honey-stomachs to capacity on each foraging expedition. In order to gain information about the collection of nectar by foragers, Free (1955d) carried out some experiments in the laboratory under controlled conditions. Worker bumblebees were starved for twenty-four hours, after which each was weighed separately, before being allowed to feed at a dish of sugar syrup. When a bee had finished feeding she was reweighed so that the amount of syrup she had taken up could be determined. Under these conditions the amount of syrup that some bees drank was equivalent to 90 per cent. of their body weight, but the average was about 50 per cent. The amount of syrup a bee drank depended to some extent on the concentration of the syrup; when it contained a high percentage of sugar, a bee tended to drink more than if the percentage was lower. Further, bees which had had as much syrup of a low concentration as they would take, would often start to drink again when offered syrup of a higher concentration. As might have been expected the larger bees took more syrup than the smaller ones, but they also managed to suck it up at a quicker rate. These results suggest that the size of a bee's load of nectar depends partly on the concentration of the nectar of the flowers she is visiting. In favourable conditions she may collect nearly her own weight of nectar. These experiments also illustrate the advantage of the way in which the necessary duties are divided amongst the bees of a colony, the larger bees generally acting as foragers and the smaller ones as house-bees.

Even nectars with very low sugar concentrations appear to taste sweet to bumblebees, as Free found that hungry individuals, who would not drink pure water, would take solutions of sucrose (cane sugar), glucose (grape sugar) or lactose in concentrations of only 2–3 per cent. But they would not drink solutions of the sugar alcohol, mannitol, even when they were relatively highly concentrated, which suggests that mannitol is tasteless to bumblebees as it also is to honeybees.

Pollen loads, like nectar loads, vary greatly in size; though once more there is a tendency for the larger bees to collect the greater loads, small bees sometimes collect relatively larger loads for their size and vice versa. The heaviest pollen loads recorded amounted to about 60 per cent. of the body-weights of the bees concerned (Clements and Long 1923, Free 1955d), although the average is probably not more than about 20 per cent.

During a single foraging trip, a worker bumblebee may either collect a load of nectar only, or a load of pollen only, or a mixed load containing both nectar and pollen. In many of these latter cases a bee may have collected a full load of one type of food but not of the other. Whilst it is quite common to find that returning foragers have collected nectar only and are carrying no pollen, about three-quarters of the bees returning home with pollen will have collected some nectar as well.

The whole question as to why some foragers collect pollen and others do not, has recently been investigated. Brian (1952), studying her *B. agrorum* colonies, discovered that whether or not a forager collected pollen was in some way dependent upon her size; the larger foragers returned home with pollen in their pollen-baskets from a higher percentage of expeditions than did smaller ones. Free (1955b) has shown that this is true in other species also. How can we explain these observations? They cannot be due to the inability of small bees to collect pollen, since even tiny ones sometimes do so, but as Brian points out, the reduced tendency for small bees to collect pollen could arise either because they visit the same flowers as the larger ones but somehow fail to collect any pollen from them, or because they visit different kinds of flowers in which there is little or no pollen to collect. There is a certain amount of evidence (Cumber 1949a) that small bees visit different kinds of flowers than the larger ones, but it seems unlikely that there is less pollen available in them. Furthermore, Free has observed several marked bees, all from the same colony, who were foraging on a patch of clover, and found that whereas some of the bees collected nectar only, others collected pollen; so it seems probable that, even when visiting the same flowers, small foragers tend to collect pollen less often than do larger ones, but at present we do not know why this should be so.

Free (1955b) followed up Brian's work by determining how constant in their behaviour individual bees were to collecting pollen or nectar. Analysis of the results of observations of the behaviour of foragers from several colonies showed that throughout a number of consecutive trips individual bees tended to remain faithful to the collection of pollen or nectar only; but when an analysis was made of the behaviour of the same individuals during several consecutive days, or during the whole period throughout which their colonies were watched, only a very few bees were found to show such constancy. The majority of foragers collected only nectar on some occasions, but returned with pollen on others. We know that when the relative humidity of the atmosphere is high, some flowers fail to open and, furthermore, pollen does not become available in others that do open, so that whether or not a given forager collects pollen during any particular trip must obviously depend to some extent on weather conditions and their influence on the availability of pollen. It also seems probable that the ratio of pollen to nectar collected by foragers is in some way related to their colony's needs—in other words that the number of larvae requiring pollen for food influences the foraging activities of the field-bees.

Let us consider the evidence in support of this. Sladen (1912) and Brian (1952) have noted that pollen sometimes continues to be brought into a colony which no longer has any larvae to feed, so it is obvious that no exact relationship exists between the presence or absence of larvae requiring food and pollen collection. However, experiments have been carried out by Free to determine whether there is a more general relationship. A pair of colonies were watched simultaneously, and the ratio of pollen to nectar loads collected by the foragers of each colony was determined. The larvae were then removed from one of the colonies and the ratio of pollen to nectar loads for each colony was again recorded. Similar observations were made with other pairs of colonies. Comparison of the ratios of pollen to nectar loads for each pair, before and after the larvae had been removed from one of them, showed that although the foragers of the colonies whose larvae had been removed still continued to collect some pollen they did not collect proportionately as much as they had been doing before their larvae were removed. It is clear, therefore, that the amount of pollen collected by the foragers of a colony is to some extent dependent on the food-requirements of its larvae.

It is interesting to consider whether the quantities of nectar and pollen in the stores of a colony also effect the proportions of these foods gathered by its foragers. Sladen was the first person to provide any information on this subject. When he fed his colonies with syrup it tended to make the bees 'lazy'; this led him to suggest that worker bumblebees may cease to forage as soon as sufficient food is available inside their nests. Recently, a number of experiments have been carried out to test this view. On several occasions Free has filled about half the available honeypots of colonies with syrup, and has subsequently noted the behaviour of the foragers of these colonies when they have returned home. In general they behaved in one of two ways. If they had previously been collecting loads of nectar, then they tended to stay inside their nest and not to go out to forage again during the next few hours; but, if, on the other hand, they had been collecting pollen, they deposited their loads in their nests and went off to collect more as usual. It appears, therefore, that the quantity of nectar or syrup that is stored in a nest determines whether or not the nectar-gatherers remain at home or go out to forage, although the possibility that individual foragers may no longer have been able to deposit their loads of nectar in particular honeypots they were accustomed to, may perhaps have contributed towards this result. The marked differences in the behaviour of the nectar and pollen-gatherers in these experiments further illustrate the constancy of foragers to collecting nectar or pollen over short periods. There was no tendency for those bees, who had been collecting nectar only, to start to gather pollen instead: but this might possibly happen if colonies are fed with syrup for long enough.

In other experiments the pollen-stores of colonies were supplemented, either by filling the storage cells of pollen-storing species with pollen, or by placing balls of pollen, about 10 mm. in diameter, on the combs of pocket-making species. Needless to say all the colonies used in these experiments had plenty of developing brood which, of course, needed pollen for its growth to continue. The addition of pollen to a colony resulted in its bees collecting relatively less pollen, and in some cases relatively more nectar, than before. This was true both of pocket-making and of pollen-storing species, and was rather surprising in the case of the pocket-making species, since their pollen-gatherers normally deposit their pellets of pollen directly into larval pockets (p. 17). It indicated that the workers had either transferred the pollen directly into the larval pockets or else had fed the larvae with regurgitated pollen. Since we know that pocket-makers can, if necessary, feed their larvae with regurgitated food the latter explanation would seem to be the more probable.

Although no critical experiments involving the removal of stores from colonies have been made, we can guess that if this were done the behaviour of the foragers would be influenced. We have seen (Chapter 6, p. 48) how the house-bees of a colony change over to foraging duties when their colony's foraging force, and thus their incoming food-supplies, becomes depleted, and Kugler (1943) found that removal of the nectar from the honey-pots of a colony encouraged its bees to go out foraging.

It seems clear, from the results of all these experiments, that whether a forager collects pollen or collects only nectar is deter-mined, to some extent at least, by the requirements of her colony. Amongst other factors these requirements depend on the nature of the stores of food within her nest and also on the age of the brood. Fluctuations in these factors no doubt partly explain the day-to-day variations in the kinds of food collected by particular foragers.

The time-lapse between a bee leaving her nest to forage and her return again, may be anything from a few minutes to several hours and depends, amongst other things, on the availability of the food she is seeking. Observations have shown that, on the average, bees returning with pollen loads take about a third as long again per trip as those who return with only nectar (Brian 1952; Free 1955d; Taniguchi 1955). The duration of a foraging trip also varies somewhat with the species concerned. For instance we find that whereas those species whose bees are rather small (e.g. *B. agrorum, B. ardens, B. pratorum* and *B. sylvarum*) generally take about twenty minutes or less to collect a load of nectar, the average duration of nectar-gathering trips of other species whose foragers are on the average larger (e.g. *B. lucorum, B. terrestris*) is over fifty minutes.

Sometimes some foragers do not return to their nests in the evening but spend the night resting on the flowers which they have been visiting. Such bees had not, apparently, collected full loads of food by the time that darkness overtook them. Free found that nearly a quarter of the foragers of a *B. lucorum* colony he was watching remained away from home at night; he attributed this relatively high proportion of the foragers who were absent to the length of time bees of this species take to collect loads of nectar and pollen.

When a laden forager returns to her nest she often appears very fastidious in her choice of a cell in which to deposit the food she has collected, and will spend some time examining one cell after another until she ultimately selects one. It is possible that during her search for a suitable cell a bee becomes 'aware' of the food requirements of her colony.

After a pollen-gatherer has found a suitable cell or larval pocket in which to place her pollen, she stands on its edge, facing away from it and inserts her hind-legs into it. Then, by a quick slicing movement with her middle pair of legs, she pushes the pollen out of her pollen-baskets into the cell. Often, just before she removes the pollen, she turns round quickly to inspect the pollen-cell again, as though to make sure that she is in the correct position for her pellets of pollen to fall into it. Having unloaded her pollen she sometimes packs it down into the cell herself, or she may go away and leave this task to be carried out by a house-bee; individual bees vary in their behaviour at different times.

Foragers who return to their nests with relatively small pollen loads as well as nectar often only deposit the nectar before going out again, still carrying their pollen with them. One particular *B. pratorum* forager flew from her nest on four consecutive occasions still carrying pollen loads which increased in size on each trip; not until the end of her fifth trip did she deposit the pollen she had collected, as well as the nectar. Other foragers have been seen to return to their nests with pollen on one leg only, the pollen on the other leg having presumably been acci- dentally lost. When this happened they did not discharge their single pellets of pollen until they had made further foraging trips and had returned with a small load of pollen in the pollen- basket which had previously been empty. It seems that the pollen loads must be of a certain size, and present on both legs, before a bee will deposit them.

When discharging a nectar load a bee stands on her chosen honeypot and inserts her head into it. Then, with rapid con- tractions of her abdomen, she forces the nectar from her honey- stomach into the honeypot. During the course of a day several of the honeypots in large nests may become filled in turn, but, in the case of small colonies at any rate, there is a tendency for the foragers to deposit their loads in only a limited number of the available honeypots, individual bees remaining fairly constant to one or two, although their choice appears to vary every few days (Brian 1952). It seems probable that nectar-gatherers prefer to deposit their loads in cells that are already partly filled, and it may be supposed that if the honeypots of a nest become empty during the night, the first load to be brought home the next morning is deposited in one chosen at random; this would account for the change in preference that has been observed.

Similar constancy to relatively few of the available pollen-cells appears to occur in nests of pollen-storing species, and foragers of pocket-making species often examine several pollen-pockets before they finally unload their pollen. The most important factor governing the choice of a pocket appears to be the stage of development of the accompanying batch of larvae, and in this case there does not seem to be a tendency for individual foragers always to deposit their loads in the same pocket.

It has been mentioned that although the amount of pollen collected is reduced when the larvae are removed from a colony, often some is still collected. When a colony of a pocket-making species has no larvae, any pollen collected by its foragers is deposited in empty cocoon-cells, as happens in the case of the pollen-storing species, and such cocoon-cells are sometimes built up with wax by the workers into tall cylindrical cups. Even when larvae and their accompanying pockets again become available in such nests some of the pollen collected may still be deposited in these cups.

Having unloaded the food she has collected, a forager will frequently rapidly clean herself and leave the nest again. Often a nectar-gatherer will only spend between 1 to 3 minutes inside her nest between trips, but if she has pollen to unload as well, she will average about a minute longer. Sometimes foragers will take a small drink of nectar before leaving again, and may carry away any debris or larvae that have been pulled out of the comb by house-bees.

Most people are now familiar with the fascinating discoveries of von Frisch concerning the dance language of the honeybee,

Plate 17.—Worker Bumblebees Feeding—*Bombus lucorum*
Bumblebees can readily be trained to collect sugar syrup. (x 1.6).

a

b

Plate 18.—A POLLEN-GATHERER—*Bombus locorum*
When approaching a flower sight guides a bee towards it; but when she is
close to it the flower's scent plays an important guiding role.
a. The approach flight (x 1·7).
b. The bee has just alighted. Note the position of the antennae, which bear the
olfactory organs (x 1·6).

and will know how a honeybee forager who has discovered a
particularly rich source of food can communicate its position to
other members of her colony by performing a 'dance' on the
surface of the comb, every now and then giving some of the
nectar she has collected to members of her colony who follow
her steps. Several observers have closely followed the behaviour
of bumblebee foragers when they return to their nests, to see if
they are in any way able to communicate to their sisters the sites of
particularly beneficial crops they have discovered. However, all
observers seem to agree that no such system of communication
exists and that no evolutionary trend in this direction can be
observed. Even when bumblebees have been trained to visit a
dish containing sugar syrup and have visited it repeatedly they
do not recruit any companions to help them collect the food.
Relatively few foragers are present in a nest during the greater
part of the day anyway, so that the ability to communicate
information concerning the position of a source of food would
probably be of limited value.

The inhabitants of a bumblebee colony take little notice of
foragers who have just returned home, though they may occasionally nibble at any pollen that they are carrying, and if nectar is
in short supply many of them drink some of it as soon as it has
been discharged into a honeypot. Only very rarely is any
food passed directly from one bumblebee to another. The eager
way in which a forager who has just returned home searches
for a suitable receptacle in which to deposit the food she has
collected may perhaps excite other members of her colony to go
out and search for food, particularly at the beginning of a day;
and when a forager leaves her nest she may perhaps help to
encourage other bees who have not flown before to do likewise.

A form of communication may exist in the field, however,
since Brian (1957) found that on visiting flowers bumblebees
show a tendency to alight on those at which other bees are
already feeding, and she suggested that the presence of a few
bees on a crop may attract newcomers to it.

CHAPTER 12

BUMBLEBEES AND FLOWERS

While Honey lies in Every Flower, no doubt,
It takes a Bee to get the Honey out.

ARTHUR GUITERMAN. *A Poet's Proverbs*

THE relationship between bees and flowers has been the source of much speculation ever since Sprengel in 1793 first drew attention to the large number of flowers that are dependent upon insects for their pollination. It is only recently, however, thanks to the patient experiments and observations of numerous workers, that we have really begun to obtain detailed information concerning those attributes of flowers to which bees respond when visiting them. Honeybees have been the favourite objects of such studies but, thanks to some notable early contributions by Charles Darwin (1876) and the recent work of Kugler (1943) and Manning (1956a, 1956b) [see also reviews by Clements and Long 1923; and Brian 1954], we now know a considerable amount about the relationships between bumblebees and flowers, and many of the gaps in our knowledge can be inferred from what we know about the honeybee.

It is well known that certain types of flowers which are irregular in shape (e.g. *Antirrhinum* spp. and *Aconitum* spp.) are particularly favoured by bumblebees, and have indeed come to be known as "bumblebee flowers". The preference shown by bumblebees for such flowers is beautifully illustrated by the observations of Leppik (1953) in the extensive flower gardens at the State Horticultural College at Weihenstephan in Bavaria where several hundreds of kinds of flowers are regularly available to insect visitors. During 1948 and 1949 he recorded 2,756 bumblebees but only 22 honeybees visiting irregularly shaped flowers, whereas he counted 2,779 honeybees and only 324 bumblebees visiting radially symmetrical flowers.

It is, in general, the petals which give a flower its characteristic appearance, and simple early experiments which involved denuding flowers of all their petals, often resulted in such flowers receiving fewer visits from bees than before, thus illustrating the importance of the petals in attracting bees to visit flowers. A notable experiment of this type was performed by Fox Wilson (1929), who went so far as to remove the petals from all the flowers of a number of Apple trees. Bumblebees then flew past without visiting them, although they worked the blossom of normal trees situated on either side.

To human beings the most striking feature of most flowers are their colours and, in a series of experiments similar to the elegant, classical ones that von Frisch had undertaken earlier on the colour vision of honeybees, Kugler tried to find out what colours, if any, bumblebees can see. He first trained some bumblebees to collect food (sugar syrup) from small tubes placed in the centre of cards of one particular colour, and then presented them with a chequerboard arrangement of cards of various colours, amongst which cards of the particular colour which he had attempted to train the bees to associate with food were included. For example he found that when he trained his bees to visit blue cards, it was on cards of this colour that most of them searched for food when he tested them with his chequerboard. Although it seemed likely from this result that the bees were seeing blue as a distinct colour, the possibility could not be excluded that they were recognising the blue cards, and distinguishing them from those of other colours, not by colour as such, but rather by their different degree of brightness. In order to overcome this difficulty Kugler performed other experiments in which his bees were offered cards not only of the colour to which he had attempted to train them but also a number of grey cards of the same degree of brightness. The bees still continued to select the coloured cards correctly, thus suggesting that bumblebees do not distinguish between coloured cards by their relative brightness, but perceive their colours as such. One cannot, however, be quite certain that this is the case until it has been shown, by successfully training them to different bands of spectral light, that they are not responding to the different amounts of ultra-violet light reflected by the cards of various colours. This has already been demonstrated in honeybees.

As a result of his experiments Kugler concluded that bumble-bees can distinguish between the colours which we call blue, green and yellow, and also, to some extent, between shades of the same colour, such as pale and dark yellow, although not as well as between the primary colours. Bumblebees appear to be red-blind, as are honeybees, since Kugler found that they are unable to distinguish between red and the darker shades of grey. Although no critical experiments appear to have been performed, it is quite likely that bumblebees, like honeybees, see ultra-violet light, which is invisible to man, as a true colour.

Although this work indicates that bumblebees can recognise the colours of flowers, it does not tell us anything about the importance of flower-colours to foraging bumblebees. Some data on this subject have been obtained by other experiments of Kugler and of Forel. Both of these investigators found that when the cards of a given colour, on which bees had become accustomed to collect food, were replaced by cards of a different colour the bees became confused and eventually flew off without alighting. Darwin (1876) whilst watching bumblebees who were exclusively visiting plants of the white-flowered *Spiranthes autumnalis* was struck by the fact that they often flew to within a few inches of the flowers of several other kinds of plants which also possessed white flowers, but without alighting on them. It seems likely, therefore, that when bees are visiting flowers of one species they become accustomed to their particular colour. This one can easily verify. If yellow and blue discs are scattered among a batch of Dandelions (*Taraxacum officinale*) the bees collecting food from the dandelions will sometimes fly down to inspect the yellow discs but will usually ignore the blue ones altogether. However, as Darwin first pointed out, bumblebees often fly directly from a flower of one colour to a differently coloured flower of the same species; for example, from a dark purple to a bright yellow Pansy, and between Polyanthus flowers of different colours. It is not surprising, therefore, that Kugler found that bumblebees can be simultaneously trained to collect food from cards of two different colours, although it is, of course, possible that when visiting flowers of the same species, but with different colours, bumblebees may pay little or no attention to the flowers' colours and concentrate more on other characteristics which the flowers have in common.

As well as studying bumblebees' colour-vision, Kugler also investigated their ability to perceive the form and shape of a flower, and he came to the general conclusion that the size of a flower, the degree of 'brokenness' or disruption of its outline, and the extent of its three-dimensional effect, are all appreciated by bumblebees and have an important influence on their responses to different kinds of flowers.

In order to investigate the effect of flower-size upon bees Kugler noted the responses of foragers to coloured discs of different sizes and found that, within limits, the larger the size of a disc the more attractive it became. For example when bees had an opportunity to choose between discs 3 cm. and 2 cm. in diameter they visited the former almost twice as often as the latter. The results of these experiments with models agree with the results obtained earlier by Clements and Long, who reduced by half the size of the petals of a large number of flowers of several different species, and found that the attractiveness of these flowers fell in practically all cases by an amount which varied from a half to a tenth. On the other hand, they found that by increasing the area of the attractive surface of a flower, they augmented the number of visits it received. For instance they found that by splitting the petals and turning back the sepals of flowers of *Aconitum* spp., thereby increasing their surface areas, they made them more than four times as attractive as normal flowers.

When we consider the degree of disruption of a flower's outline—the extent of its silhouette—Kugler's bees definitely seemed to show a preference for complex rather than simple configurations. When he tested the reactions of bees to circular discs and star-shaped ones, and to 6-rayed stars and 12-rayed ones, the more broken-up figures were preferred. More recent work (Leppik 1953) has even indicated that within limits bees may be able to recognise the number of petals which a flower possesses.

Finally Kugler investigated the relative attractiveness of

three-dimensional and two-dimensional models, by offering the bees a choice of models half of which were cone-shaped and half flat discs of the same diameter as the open ends of the cones. Both types of model were mounted on wire 'stalks'. The three-dimensional models proved by far the more attractive and received as many as 92 per cent of the visits, the bees forcing their way into them as far as possible. These results imply that bumble-bees prefer flowers with depth, to those without; we shall see later some of the probable biological reasons for this preference.

Apart from their colours and shapes most flowers possess a characteristic scent which is produced in or near their nectaries, and often also by their petals. In a long series of experiments Kugler has shown that bees readily learn to associate particular scents with food. In one such experiment bees were trained to collect food from models scented with rose-water, and were then offered the choice between models scented with rose-water and others 'scented' with tap water. Although bees flew towards both types of model equally they only alighted and fed on the rose-scented ones. In another experiment models scented with clove-oil, instead of tap-water, were provided during the testing time, but the bees still chose the rose-scented models to which they had been trained. This was not simply because the bees preferred the scent of rose-water to that of clove-oil since, in later experiments, bees were trained to feed from models scented with clove-oil and then preferred these to rose scented models.

Kugler also showed that, as with colours, bees can even be trained to two different scents simultaneously. He found that bees who had previously been conditioned to visit some models scented with clove-oil, and others scented with acetone, subsequently selected models bearing either of these two scents in preference to others bearing one of three other kinds of scent.

Scent is, undoubtedly, of far greater importance in a bumble-bee's life than it is in our own, and bumblebees have been shown readily to recognise the scent of flowers such as Toad-flax (*Linaria vulgaris*) and Viper's Bugloss (*Echium vulgare*) which most human beings cannot smell.

Having discussed some of the features of flowers to which bumblebees respond, let us now consider how bees find flowers in the field, and thereby any food they contain. Although a bee probably can be attracted by scent from some distance away to large masses of flowers that are growing close together, as in Heather moors or in cultivated crops such as Clovers, Beans or fruit-trees, a bee needs to be fairly close to an individual flower before she is able to distinguish it from its background. Both Wagner (1907) and Kugler have found that the distance at which bees first recognise a flower by sight depends on the size of the individual flower, or of the inflorescence of which it forms a part. For instance the average distance at which bees flew directly towards a model flower which was 23 mm. in diameter, was 20 cm., whereas a model that was 13 mm. in diameter was perceived at about half this distance. The distance from which a bee could recognise a model also depended on its shape. Discs like regular flowers with a few conspicuous radial petals were recognised at nearly twice the distance as circular ones. These findings undoubtedly help to explain why the attractiveness of a flower depends both upon its size and the degree to which its outline is disrupted.

Bees who are accustomed to work the flowers of a particular species of plant will probably only react to flowers of their colour, shape and size; when a bee has recognised a flower her flight towards it seems to be directed entirely by sight, scent playing little or no part. Kugler was able to demonstrate this fact by means of a very neat experiment. He placed a tall glass cylinder, open at each end, around a plant of Betony (*Stachys officinalis*), so that the scent of the flowers could only escape from the opening at the top of the cylinder. He then found that approaching bees did not fly to the top of the cylinder, but to the middle where they could see the flowers. This beautifully illustrates the importance of sight over scent when a bumblebee is flying towards a flower.

However, once a bee has approached a flower closely, the scent of the flower has an important role to play, and seems to be the most important stimulus in causing the bee actually to alight on the flower. Once a bee has become accustomed to visiting flowers, or models, with a particular scent she is easily put off, either if she does not smell any scent or smells a wrong one. Clements and Long performed numerous experiments in which artificial flowers made of crepe paper were attached to flowering plants. It appears that although bumblebees often approached these 'flowers', and inspected them closely, they rarely alighted upon them, apparently because they were unscented. They also added strange scents to flowers of numerous species, and found that this cut down the number of visits by bees to almost half. Similarly Kugler found that, when he placed drops of clove-oil on flowers of Field Scabious (*Knautia arvensis*) bees approached them closely but did not enter them. The addition of an odour where there was none before appears to have a similar effect, since Free once replaced with honey the sugar syrup in artificial flowers on which bees were foraging, and found that subsequently the bees hesitated to alight on them, although no one would doubt that honey is normally attractive to them.

Early experiments by Plateau (1902) and Forel (1908) are of interest in this connection. They cut off the antennae (which bear many organs, including those of smell) of some bumblebees who were visiting flowers of Bindweed (*Convolvulus* spp.), and found that many of these mutilated bees still continued to visit them. The loss of their antennae seemed, if anything, to increase the precision with which they flew from flower to flower and, instead of hovering briefly in front of a flower before alighting upon it, as they had done before, they now made a 'bee line' for it and alighted immediately.

Little work has been done to discover those features of flowers to which bees react on their very first foraging flights, and such an investigation would be well worth undertaking. Kugler did find, however, that when on their 'maiden voyages' bumblebees showed an innate tendency to examine his coloured models, but that there is no such inborn tendency for bees to respond to flower-scents. It seems, therefore, that it is only after bees have become accustomed to visiting the flowers of a particular species of plant and have learned their scent, that the latter assumes importance in eliciting further visits.

Although, once she starts visiting the flowers of a given species a bee soon learns the position of their nectaries relative to their petals etc., one may ask how a bee knows whereabouts to find the nectaries of a species of flower which she is visiting for the first time. Here again both sight and scent may help her.

Sprengel, in his great work to which we referred at the beginning of this chapter, called attention to the fact that the petals of many flowers possess a series of spots or lines of contrasting colours (especially from a bee's point of view) and he suggested that these patterns guide insects to the nectaries. He also noted that these so-called "nectar-guides" are more commonly found in flowers of irregular shape, and he connected this with the fact that the nectaries of irregularly shaped flowers are probably more difficult for bees to find than those of regularly shaped ones. Sprengel's views were not universally accepted, and Darwin (1841) himself questioned whether such spots and streaks on many nectiferous flowers do actually serve as guides. Recently, however, thanks to the careful work of Manning, experimental evidence has been obtained which shows that such nectar-guides do in effect guide bumblebees to the nectaries.

Although Kugler had earlier concluded that when flowers are radially symmetrical foraging bees instinctively make for their centres, Manning, by making use of an improved method of recording visits, showed that bees visiting circular discs, star-shaped discs, or discs shaped like regular flowers with a few conspicuous radial petals, on which no food was provided, usually reacted to the edges of these models and rarely to their centres, even though the centres of the two latter types of model were defined by virtue of their shape. When, however, Manning introduced artificial nectar-guides to his models, by adding a series of lines of contrasting colour radiating outwards from their centres, the flying bees dipped down towards the centres of the models nearly twice as often as they did to their edges. In other experiments Manning had shown there is a tendency for bees to follow lines which contrast in colour with their background, so it seems that the above results were obtained because the bees followed the nectar-guides from the edges to the centres of the models.

An isolated observation made by Free on the behaviour of a *B. lapidarius* queen when she had just arrived at a bed of Wall-flowers (*Cheiranthus cheiri*) is perhaps relevant. When visiting her first flower the queen extended her tongue and pushed it along a nectar-guide from the edge of the petal until it reached the nectary. She repeated this performance on the next three flowers she visited but, when on the fifth and subsequent flowers she inserted her tongue directly into their nectaries. It is possible, therefore, that nectar-guides are of great importance in helping a bee to find the nectary of flowers of a particular kind on the first few occasions she visits them, but soon become less important after she has visited them a few times and learned the positions of their nectaries.

Manning found that not only did the models with nectar-guides attract bees to their centres, but also that the bees hovered in the air around the models which possessed such guides for longer periods than around models without them, even when no food was provided in either type. This agrees well with an earlier observation of Kugler, who found that when his bees were allowed to choose between plain circular discs and circular discs with nectar-guides painted on them, both provided with food, the bees alighted upon and fed from the latter much more frequently. It is possible, therefore, that apart from their directing function, the presence of nectar-guides on a flower may also increase its general attractiveness to bees or make recognition easier.

We have already seen how bees prefer to alight and feed on cone-shaped in preference to disc-like models of flowers. Manning observed that although the bees primarily reacted to the edge of both types, only in the case of the cone-shaped models did the bees subsequently react towards their centres. He concluded that the 'depth' of a cone-shaped model is attractive and acts in the same sort of way as a nectar-guide in directing bees to the model's centre. The effect of depth, seems to depend on deepening shade, as was clearly demonstrated in a subsequent experiment. Manning tested bumblebees' reactions to flat circular discs that were painted the same colour all over and to other discs that were painted in such a way that the colour gradated toward the centre, thus giving a false visual impression of depth, the shade of colour at the margins of the discs being equivalent to that of the plain discs. He found that the bees responded much more towards the centres of the shaded models than towards those of the unshaded ones.

Apart from scent being important as a means of flower identification, it probably also plays an important part in guiding bees to the nectaries of flowers, as it is likely that a gradient of scent extends outwards from them. Some evidence in favour of this view was obtained by Manning, who showed that the presence of a drop of scent (lavender) in the middle of a model attracted the bees towards its centre. It has recently been shown (Lex 1954) that parts of the petals of flowers smell differently, or more intensively, than others. It seems that, quite apart from visible nectar-guides, flowers may also possess scent-guides and that these may well be of even greater importance to insects who are, perhaps, better fitted to differentiate between different scents and to follow scent gradients than to distinguish between different colours.

For the most part we have so far been discussing conspicuous flowers, but many inconspicuous flowers, of which Contoneaster (*C. integerrinus*), Alder (*Alnus glutinosa*) and Willow (*Salix* spp.) are good examples, are often freely visited by bumblebees. Although the size, colour and shape of the petals of flowers are undoubtedly factors which help to elicit the initial visits of bees, it must not be forgotten that the amount and concentration of nectar, and the amount of pollen available, as well as numerous other ecological factors, will ultimately decide the attention they receive.

An early observation by Darwin (1876) indicated, that apart from the flowers themselves, bees are sometimes able to recognise the general form of a plant. He saw bumblebees flying from a Larkspur (*Delphinium* spp.), which was in full flower, to another Larkspur plant fifteen yards away which had not a single flower open. Since the buds on this latter plant were only a faint tinge of blue, the optical stimuli must have come from the plant itself, and recent experiments of Manning's have indeed confirmed that bumblebees can sometimes recognise a plant's general form.

When working Hound's-tongue (*Cynoglossum officinale* L.), a tall plant with rather inconspicuous flowers, the bees soon become conditioned to the general form of the plant because the flowers themselves are of little use in guiding them. Thus bees regularly visiting hound's-tongue will also search plants without flowers belonging to another species with approximately the same general form and shape as hound's-tongue plants, as well as any hound's-tongue plants which are not in flower, or from which the flowers have been removed. On the other hand, bees visiting Foxgloves (*Digitalis purpurea*) which, of course, have large conspicuous flowers, are attracted entirely by the flowers themselves, and apparently do not learn the general form of the plant. In direct contrast to bees visiting hound's-tongue, bees that are working foxgloves will not even react to flowerless foxglove plants, let alone plants of other species which resemble the foxglove in general form. Manning supposed that between these two extremes one can expect to find a long range of intermediates where both the flowers and the plant-form play their parts in different proportions. These results illustrate how bumblebees, when visiting different plant species, can readily adapt themselves to learn very different features of the plants concerned.

In conclusion a word must be said about the peculiar habit, for which certain species of bumblebees have become infamous, of making holes near to the nectaries of long tubular flowers. Some species make these holes by biting through the corollae with their mandibles, whilst others pierce them with their tongues. Through these holes they, and bumblebees of other species, and even honeybees, who follow them, can insert their tongues and therefore obtain nectar without conferring any advantage on the plant. Over 300 species of flowers are known from which nectar is obtained in this manner (Lovell 1918); typical examples are Monkshood (*Aconitum anglicum*), Scarlet Runner Bean (*Phaseolus coccineus*), Heather (*Erica* spp.) Red Clover (*Trifolium pratense*), Toadflax (*Linaria vulgaris*) and Gentians (*Gentiana* spp.).

How can we explain this habit? Darwin suggested that, although when making the perforations bees are likely to work more slowly than usual, such bees may, nevertheless, be working for the good of their communities by enabling other members of them who come along later to collect nectar more efficiently and quickly by making use of the holes. In support of this view he pointed out that bees whom he saw obtaining nectar through holes already made in flowers of *Stachys* spp. and *Pentstemon* spp., were able to work nearly twice as quickly as they would have done had they entered these flowers in the usual way.

A more likely explanation was put forward by Knuth (1906). He realised that those species that are most prone to make such holes all possess relatively short tongues in comparison with the rest of the bumblebees. Consequently he suggested that when bees of these short-tongued species are unable to reach the nectar in long tubular flowers in the normal way they resort to biting. Although many bumblebee species have been recorded as biting holes at some time or another, the species most prone to adopt this habit (*B. lucorum, B. mastrucatus* and *B. terrestris* in Europe, and *B. affinis* and *B. terricola* in America) are all relatively short-tongued species (See review by Brian 1954).

Kugler, however, considered that Knuth's hypothesis had a serious drawback. Why, he argued, if short-tongued bumblebees bite holes in flowers in which the nectar is available to long-tongued bumblebees, do not long-tongued bumblebees, such as *B. hortorum*, bite holes in flowers whose nectaries are normally only available to butterflies with their still longer tongues? Instead Kugler himself suggested that if a bee is unable to obtain nectar by the normal method she will explore the flower until she comes across a weak spot through which she can bite or force her tongue. He considered that only certain species of bumble-bees possess mouth-parts that are strong enough to do this, and mentioned that *B. mastrucatus*, the most notorious of all for this habit, has very powerful mandibles. On the other hand he regarded the mouth-parts of *B. hortorum* as being very weak, so that she is unable to make holes in flowers which have corolla tubes that are so long that even she with her long tongue is unable to reach their nectaries.

However, recent work by Brian (1957) has shown that individual bumblebee species do not visit some kinds of flowers whose corolla-length is such that their nectaries are well within the reach of the bumblebees' tongues, so, whether or not bees visit a particular species of flower is certainly not determined solely by the relative lengths of their tongues and of the corolla tubes of the flowers concerned. Moreover, flowers with such deep corolla tubes that their nectaries cannot be reached by *B. hortorum* are comparatively rare, whereas there are many flowers whose corolla tubes are too long to permit the so-called robbing species from obtaining nectar in the normal way, and it is probably not too rash to suggest that the acquisition of this habit, which was only possible on account of their powerful mouth-parts, has probably played an important role in the survival of such species.

Finally, how does a bee find whereabouts to bite a flower? It appears that at first a bee will often pierce many different parts of a flower before she succeeds in reaching its nectaries, and Schremmer (1955) believes that when she visits the next flower of the same kind she remembers the position which she occupied on the previous one and, by adopting this same position, she is correctly orientated to bite a hole close to the nectaries of the new flower.

We have said nothing in this chapter on that most important aspect of the bee/flower relationship, the pollination of fruit and seed crops, as we consider it in detail in Chapter 15, p. 130.

CHAPTER 13

FORAGING

The wild bee reels from bough to bough
With his furry coat and his gauzy wing,
Now in a lily-cup and now
Setting the jacinth bell a-swing.

OSCAR WILDE. *Her Voice*

WE now turn to a consideration of the general foraging behaviour of bumblebees rather than their reactions to individual flowers.

Bumblebees have gained the reputation of continuing to work in the field under weather conditions in which honeybees remain at home. In 1929 Fox Wilson published the results of five years, observations which showed that bumblebees will continue to forage on fruit blossom during dull and overcast weather, cold winds, high winds and gales, during heavy and continuous rain, and even during snow and hail showers! He does mention, however, that during wet and windy weather he found them less active and sometimes crawling from flower to flower with great deliberation, an observation corroborated by Pittioni (1937).

At the time of year at which Fox Wilson made his observations by far the greater part of the population consisted of young queens, and Løken (1949) has confirmed that, in Norway, the activity of such young queens is little affected even by heavy showers. In general it seems true to say that rain has much less effect on the foraging population at the beginning of the season than it does at the end (Hulkkonen 1928 and Løken 1949), and it has been suggested that at this former time, when the small rapidly developing colonies often have little or nothing in the way of food-reserves, the urgency to collect food is much greater.

This is likely to be particularly so in the case of a colony whose brood is still being looked after by the queen alone.

Not only do bumblebees work in more inclement weather at the beginning of the season than they do at the end, but they also often work for longer hours. Hulkkonen observed that early in the season bumblebees continue to forage until about an hour after sunset, whereas from the end of July to mid-August they only do so until about sunset, and later still in the season they return home long before sunset.

Hulkkonen came to the conclusion that as night approaches and the light-intensity diminishes bumblebees tend to visit flowering trees and shrubs rather than low-growing flowers, and also white flowers in preference to coloured ones, presumably because they can see them more readily. However, Løken found that late in the evening bumblebees may continue to visit the same kind of flowers as they have worked earlier in the day, and she recorded an instance of them visiting the dark reddish-purple flowers of Hedge-Woundwort (*Stachys silvatica*) some two hours after sunset, when it was already so dark that she had to capture the foragers and take them into a lighted room before she could identify them. It has been reported by Longstaff (1932) that bumblebees fly all through the light summer nights in the Arctic, and Hulkkonen has recorded them flying by moonlight in India.

During the solar eclipse which took place soon after mid-day on 30th June 1954 Løken recorded the behaviour of foraging bumblebees at Bergen in Norway. She found that the number of bees foraging decreased rapidly just before totality occurred, by which time all except one had disappeared from the raspberry bushes she was observing. Nearly 10 minutes elapsed after the eclipse was over before any bees returned to the Raspberries to forage once more. Her data agree with the fact that bees will only start foraging in the morning at a light-intensity considerably higher than that at which they will continue foraging in the

---

Plate 19 (opposite). FORAGING BUMBLEBEES. A.
The long-tongued species of Bumblebees are important pollinators of red clover and other crops.
above. B. *agrorum* worker on red clover (x 2·2)
below. B. *hortorum* worker, another long-tongued species of economic importance, on a cornflower (x 2·1)

Plate 19

evening. As she indicated, however, it is not possible to correlate the beginning and end of foraging for the day with any single factor of the environment, since several factors, such as light-intensity, temperature and humidity are all closely interrelated. Both high and low temperatures can limit foraging, and Løken (1949) found that foraging sometimes ceases in the middle of the day if the temperature is high while continuing unaffected in the cooler mountain regions.

Both Free (1955d) and Taniguchi (1955) have found that although the proportion of the workers that go foraging is relatively stable during the greater part of the day, it steadily increases during the first few hours of morning and steadily decreases during the last few hours of evening, thus indicating a wide variation in the conditions under which individual bees will begin and end their foraging. Free once saw a worker fly from her nest carrying a larva several minutes after all the other foragers of her colony had completed their last trips of the day. Some ten minutes later this same bee returned to her nest carrying a load of pollen, so that although all the other members of her colony had stopped foraging for the night, this was not because it was impossible to gather food. It may be that when the nest temperature falls below a certain level the foragers tend to remain at home, thus increasing the home-population which helps to maintain a relatively high nest temperature (Chapter 3, p. 24).

During the hours when foraging is most active about a third, or a little more, of a colony's population will be away from the nest at any one time. The number of trips made by individuals in a day varies greatly however. For instance, Free found that the number of trips some *B. sylvarum* foragers made varied from 1 to 27 trips per day each, and that some *B. lucorum* foragers, who tended to spend longer away from home on each occasion, made 1 to 17 trips each per day.

Plate 20 (opposite). FORAGING BUMBLEBEES. B.
Some of the earlier nesting species are important pollinators of raspberries and other fruit.
above. *B. pratorum* worker foraging on a raspberry flower (x 1·7)
below. *B. pratorum* male. Male bumblebees, unlike drone honeybees, forage for themselves and so help to pollinate flowers (x 1·4)

It is interesting to note that whenever a comparison has been made of the number of flowers which bumblebees and honeybees visit in a given time it has nearly always been found that the bumblebees were working nearly two or even three times as quickly. The working rate of bumblebees varies in different species; to quote two recently published examples, Skovgaard (1952) recorded *B. agrorum* as working faster than *B. lapidarius* or *B. terrestris* when foraging on Red Clover, and Thies (1953) found that although *B. americanorum* on the average visits about five Cotton flowers per minute *B. auricomus* visited only about three in the same period.

It has long been known that different species of bumblebees show decided preferences for different species of flowers. Sladen (1912), Laidlaw (1930) and Yarrow (1943) each give examples of the favourite flowers of the different species in this country, and Fye and Medler (1954a) have done the same thing for American bumblebees. This preference for different kinds of flowers is well illustrated by some recent work of Brian (1951b) who studied, by an ingenious method, the sources of pollen collected by workers of colonies of *B. agrorum*, *B. hortorum* and *B. lucorum* in the West of Scotland. She identified the different kinds of pollen present in the faeces which larval bumblebees eject just before pupating. These faeces are deposited as a hard mass on the outside of each cocoon, and the 'shells' of the pollen grains in each mass represent all the pollen that a particular larva has eaten during its life. By identifying the pollen grains present, with the aid of a microscope, she was able to obtain a very good idea of the source of the pollen supplies of the colonies to which the larvae belonged. Although the colonies of the three species mentioned were all situated in the same locality, there were considerable differences in the kinds of pollen present in each case. *B. agrorum* had obtained their pollen mainly from Red Clover (*Trifolium pratense*), White Clover (*Trifolium repens*), Bird's-foot Trefoil (*Lotus corniculatus*) and a Vetch (*Vicia* spp.); *B. lucorum* colonies principally from white clover and Heathers (*Ericaceae* spp.), and *B. hortorum* mainly from red clover.

The latest work of Brian (1957) sheds some further light on this subject and indicates that, although it is possible that other factors are also involved, the choice of different kinds of flowers by the various species of bumblebees is associated with the depth of their corolla tubes and with the bees' preferences for foraging in different sorts of places. For example, *B. lucorum* tends only to visit flowers with very short corolla tubes, and *B. pratorum* mainly visits flowers with such shallow tubes, whilst *B. hortorum* restricts its visits to flowers with deep corolla tubes, and *B. agrorum* to flowers with corolla tubes intermediate in length. Whilst *B. lucorum* visits flowers in exposed places such as open fields, moorland, the tops of hedges and high trees, *B. agrorum* and *B. pratorum* seem to restrict their foraging mainly to sheltered situations such as the hedge-bottoms, gardens, thickets and places where there is tall vegetation.

Ever since Aristotle first drew attention to the fact that honeybees are, in general, faithful to one particular species of flower on any one foraging trip, observations have steadily accumulated concerning their so-called 'flower-constancy'. The flower-constancy of bumblebees has not been studied to the same extent, but such information as we have indicates that bumble-bees are somewhat less constant to one species of flower during a single foraging expedition than are honeybees. Unfortunately, however, few direct comparisons have been made of the constancy shown by bumblebees and honeybees respectively whilst both are working the same kind of flower. We shall only consider the constancy shown by bumblebees during single foraging expeditions since the information we have on their constancy during successive trips is too scanty.

There are two ways of studying the flower-constancy of bees. The first, and most obvious, is simply to observe individual foragers for as long as possible and thus to determine the number of different kinds of flowers each of them visits. Observations of this type have been undertaken by Bennet (1883) and Christy (1883). Of the 84 bumblebees they followed, 52 (i.e. 62 per cent.) kept to one kind of flower during observation.

A second method, which has been used more extensively in recent years, has been to analyse pollen loads taken from indivi-dual bees and to find the number of different kinds of pollen-grains present in them. The results of five such investigations are tabulated below:

	No bees examined	% bees with pure loads
Betts (1920b)	14	59
Clements and Long (1923)	102	59
Brittain and Newton (1933)	85	57
Brian (1952)	120	44
Brian (1954)	46	65

From these figures it is evident that just under half of the bees had visited more than one species of plant during the collection of their pollen loads. But in well over half of the 'mixed' loads collected by Clements and Long over 90 per cent. of the pollen grains were of one species, and many of the mixed loads examined by Brian also had one type of pollen grain as their major consti-tuent. Such loads can hardly be regarded as evidence of a high degree of inconstancy. Furthermore, in many of the mixed loads it is probable that the different types of pollen were in separate layers not all mixed together, the bees concerned having visited one species of flower exclusively at first and later transferred their entire attention to another.

As Brittain and Newton pointed out, the degree of constancy a bee exhibits is governed largely by the availability and number of kinds of flowers present in a given place, and estimates of constancy by both the above methods suffer from the obvious disadvantage that the results obtained depend on the locality in which the bees are foraging. If they are foraging in a garden in which there are many different species of flowers, but too few of any one kind to afford adequate pasturage, a much lower degree of constancy is likely to result than in an area where one species of flower predominates, especially if this is a favourite with the species of bumblebee concerned.

One may ask what advantage a bee derives by confining her attention to one species of flower? It does not seem possible to improve upon the answer given by Darwin. We know that bees visiting flowers of a species that is new to them often have difficulty in finding the nectaries and take some time to learn where they are situated; this led Darwin (1876) to suggest that the constancy bees show for particular species of flowers enables them to work faster, since they will soon learn "how to stand in the best position on the flower, and how far and in what direction to insert their proboscis".

Since the various species of bumblebees show decided preferences for foraging in different sorts of situations, it would not be surprising if some exhibit a greater degree of flower-constancy than others. Although the constancy shown by bees of all the species whose foraging preferences have been described by Brian has not yet been measured, such a difference does occur between *B. agrorum* and *B. pratorum*, foragers of the former being more constant to one species of flower. Clements and Long also found a difference in the constancy of the American species they studied, and Pohjakallio (1938) observed that whereas *B. distinguendus* foragers rarely forsook the flowers of one species for another, *B. agrorum* did so more frequently.

Little is known about the distance from the nest that bumblebees will fly in search of food, but Rau (1924) has obtained a few data on this subject. He removed bees from their nests and liberated them at various distances; only 4 out of 19 released 1½ miles away, managed to return home again. However, it is quite possible that the majority of the bees he used had never flown before. In similar homing experiments Free only used bees captured as they returned to their nests. He found that 18 out of 20 foragers of a *B. agrorum* colony which he liberated at a distance of 500 yds. or less from their nest managed to return home, but only 2 of 9 foragers liberated at 700 or 900 yds. away. The foraging range of members of a *B. lapidarius* colony appeared to be greater, all 9 bees liberated at distances up to 1,300 yds. from their home returning to it; at greater distances the proportion of successful returns fell markedly, although one bee managed to return home from a distance of 1,800 yds.

Although these simple experiments do give a rough estimate of the foraging range of a bumblebee, it must be remembered that, as we shall see in a moment, a bee may be familiar with the territory for several hundred yards on one side of her nest but know comparatively little about the country on the other side of it, so that when such a bee is liberated even a short distance away in the latter direction she may become completely lost. In any case it only takes a forager a few minutes at the most to fly from her nest to her foraging area, since Darwin (1876) and

Schröder (1912) have shown that they fly at a speed of between 7 and 12 miles an hour.

It is probably true to say that most, if not all, foraging animals which have definite 'homes', do not forage indiscriminately over the surrounding countryside but, for some time at least, restrict their activities to comparatively small parts of the areas available to them. This is certainly true of the honeybee, and information about the bumblebee in this respect, although comparatively scanty, points to the same conclusion. Brian (1952), for example, noted the direction in which bees of a *B. agrorum* colony flew when they left their nests to forage, and was able to distinguish five main flight-paths. Individual bees tended to keep to one or other of these routes, thus suggesting that each bee was foraging consistently in the same area.

When a colony is foraging on a crop covering a large area many individual bees also probably tend to keep to their own restricted foraging areas. On one occasion Free marked 30 bees which were foraging on a patch of red clover 20 square yards in area which he had marked out near the edge of a large field. During incidental observations in the next few days 10 of these bees were seen and recaptured inside this restricted area, and 3 more a few yards outside it.

In another experiment Free studied the foraging areas of *B. agrorum* workers who were visiting a plot of red clover half an acre in extent. He placed a small colony on each of its four sides and another in the middle, and marked the members of each colony distinctively. During the next five days the positions in the plot at which the foraging bees of each colony were seen were recorded whilst walking over the crop along a predetermined course which took about an hour to cover. In general there was a tendency for bees to forage near to their nests but, whereas some bees mostly kept to relatively small areas of the crop, others were of a more roving disposition. Later observations, by Braun et al (1956) in Canada, have shown that whereas in small clover fields the bumblebees are more or less evenly dispersed over the crop, in large fields the number of bees decreases from the edges of the fields towards their centres. Since the majority, if not all, of the bumblebees they observed came from nests which were almost certainly located outside the clover fields themselves, this also indicates that bumblebees prefer to forage on those parts of the crop which are nearest to their nests and do not wander all over it at random.

Other observations made by Free on bumblebees who were visting the flowers of a continuous row of rhododendron bushes some 60 yards long, and others who were visiting a field of brassica flowers, indicate that many bees restrict their foraging to particular limited areas, to which they tend to keep on consecutive trips. But it should be pointed out that the size of a bee's foraging area, and her constancy to any particular area, is probably greatly influenced by the attractiveness of the crop concerned. Attempts were made to investigate the constancy of marked bumblebees to each of five separate beds of wallflowers. However, the wallflowers were obviously not very attractive, since no bees foraged on them consistently and many visited only one or two flowers before departing. It is not surprising, therefore, that in this case the individual bees showed little or no tendency to restrict their activities to particular beds of flowers, since it has been clearly shown that honeybees exhibit a more wandering habit when the crop they are working begins to lose its attractiveness.

Further, although one can fairly readily plot the foraging areas of those bees who return to a crop one is observing, one has no knowledge at all of the foraging areas of the bees which fail to return. This applies especially to foraging queens in springtime, since we do not even know whether queens that have not yet established nests for themselves keep somewhere near their hibernation sites or whether they travel long distances before founding their colonies.

It is unfortunate that no numerical data are available by which one can compare directly the tendencies of bumblebees and honeybees to keep to restricted foraging areas, but it seems fairly certain that bumblebees are less inclined to do so. The behaviour of foraging bumblebees is rather more difficult to observe than that of honeybees, as they are inclined to be more 'nervous' when an observer is nearby. Especially when working crops which are more than one or two feet high, bumblebees are very apt to take flight when an observer moves, and often

buzz in a seemingly ferocious manner around his head for a few
seconds before finally departing.

Not only do bumblebees sometimes restrict their visits to
definite foraging areas on a more or less homogeneous crop but,
when the plants are fairly widely separated, they may even
learn their individual positions. Darwin was the first to make such
an observation, and Manning (1956b) has recently further
examined this problem. He arranged some hound's-tongue
plants, which he had grown in pots, in such a way that they
formed two groups: a 'central' group in which the plants were
separated from one another by 6 feet or less, and an outer, more
'distal', group in which all the plants were more than 10 ft. from
each other and also from any plant in the central group. Once
bees were foraging on them regularly Manning studied the
effect of removing individual plants. When he removed a plant
from the outer group the bees still continued to visit the place
where the plant had been just as frequently as the remaining
plants. They would hover around the empty site for several
seconds, and sometimes continued to return to it on several
subsequent trips.

On the other hand, when he removed a plant from the central
group its site received fewer visits in comparison with those to
neighbouring plants, and, furthermore, those bees who did visit
the site hovered over it for a few seconds only. Thus the positions
of the plants forming the central group were certainly not as well
learnt by the bees as those of the distal group. Further evidence
in support of this conclusion was obtained. Whilst foraging on
plants in the central group the bees appeared to fly rather
uncertainly from one plant to another and, although they seemed
to know the approximate positions of the plants, they apparently
relied to a considerable extent upon direct stimulation from the
plants themselves to guide them; but when visiting individual
plants in the distal group the bees flew directly and unhesitatingly
from plant to plant and seemed to be thoroughly acquainted with
the position of each.

Manning also carried out similar experiments using foxgloves,
and found that here again the bees had an extensive knowledge
of the position of each of the plants in the distal group, but little
knowledge of those in the central group. However, the bees

seemed to have somewhat less knowledge of the positions of the foxglove plants both in the inner and outer groups than had been the case with hound's-tongue plants, and he thought that this might be correlated with the greater distance from which a bee can recognise a foxglove.

When visiting plants in the outer group a bee often developed a definite route which she followed on subsequent trips, although during some trips she would deviate from it for a short time and explore the terrain on either side. Individual bees will in some cases even follow a similar route on consecutive foraging trips when working a crop of flowers growing close together. Free plotted the path taken by a particular *B. agrorum* forager during four complete foraging expeditions in a field of red clover. On each occasion she began to forage in approximately the same direction and followed the same general, approximately circular, path until she arrived back at her nest. It seems fairly certain that when visiting an extensive crop of flowers bees do not forage at random but tend to move from flower to flower in one definite direction, for some time at least. This is likely to be especially well marked with crops planted in definite rows. Near the end of a trip the behaviour of a forager sometimes becomes erratic, however, and when she leaves a flower, instead of moving to another one close by, she may fly off and visit one or two several feet away before returning home laden with food, for which she may have had to visit several hundred flowers.

CHAPTER 14

LOCALITY LEARNING

Oft have I wondered at the faultless skill
With which thou trackest out thy dwelling cave,
Winging thy way with seeming careless will,
From mount to plain, o'er lake and winding wave.

THOMAS SMIBERT. *To the Wild Bee*

THE first time one sees worker bumblebees entering and leaving their nest in their characteristic rapid way one wonders how they know the position of the entrance to their home so well. The answer is really very simple: when a worker bumblebee leaves her nest for the first time she does not rush out but is very hesitant, carefully memorizing its position. On leaving the nest itself, the bee makes her way to the end of the entrance tunnel and then retraces her steps, repeating this manoeuvre several times until she is familiar with the lay-out of the entrance tunnel; then, and then only, she flies a short distance from the entrance, turning to face it whilst slowly rising into the air and flying in a series of gradually widening circles and zig-zags. As the circles increase in diameter and more territory is covered the bee no longer faces towards her nest and her flight grows swifter until, after about half a minute or so, she flies right away into the fields. She repeats the same procedure on subsequent excursions from her nest, but on each occasion spends less time orientating herself to her surroundings until, eventually, she flies straight away from the nest directly she emerges from its entrance. A similar and very careful orientation flight is also carried out by a queen when she first leaves a newly discovered nest-site in spring.

It has already been mentioned (p. 36) that the males of many species of bumblebees rarely, if ever, return to the nests in which they were reared, and it is interesting to note that they do not carry out orientation flights like those of the queens and workers when leaving their nests (Frison 1930; Free 1955e). On the other hand, young queens, like overwintered ones who have just discovered suitable nest-sites, do orientate themselves to the positions of their nests, and it is possible that they remember their positions for a very long time since Hoffer (1886), Frison (1930) and Plath (1934) have each observed young queens, who had only recently left their hibernating quarters, searching in places where there had been nests during the previous season.

Under natural conditions, of course, a worker bumblebee only has to learn the general position of her home once, and this suffices for the rest of her life since the position of her home does not change.

In 1908, Forel described the difficulties that bumblebees had in learning the position of their nest when he placed it on a window-ledge. He thought that this was because its location was too far removed from natural conditions, and concluded that "we are asking too much of a poor little insect-brain when we play it such tricks".

Later observers have found that bumblebees can generally reorientate themselves successfully when their nests are placed in such novel situations; to give but one example, Rau (1924) was amazed to find how accurately and how quickly bees learned the position of their nest when he placed it outside a third storey window of a house that was very like its neighbours. It is interesting to see just how adaptable worker bumblebees are in re-orientating themselves when their colony is moved to a new site, a circumstance totally outside their normal experience.

In one such experiment Free (1955e) moved a nest to a new position several miles away from its old site, so that the bees of the colony could have had no previous experience of the area in which they found themselves. On leaving their nest for the first time at the new site, all the bees flew around orientating themselves, for periods ranging from 9 to 50 seconds, before flying off, and the great majority (92 per cent) managed to return home again.

Having established that bumblebees can readily reorientate

themselves to their nest when it is placed in strange surroundings, Free decided to see how they would manage when their nest was transferred to a new position in terrain they already knew. First of all the effect of a minor alteration in the position of the entrance to a nest was investigated. The nest used was in position behind a screen (see p. 159) and the entrance to it was moved overnight so that it was displaced only 3 ins. to one side of its original position, where an empty nest-box and entrance tunnel had been placed. Two-thirds of the bees that flew the next morning made orientation flights; those that did not had presumably failed to notice any change in the relative position of the entrance. Although all the bees eventually managed to find their way back to the new site, those that had not orientated themselves when they left took much longer to do so, and it appears that they eventually found the new site more or less accidentally by searching about in the vicinity of the old one. One supposes that similar searching behaviour must often enable returning foragers to find the entrances to their nests under natural conditions, when wind or rain has disturbed the vegetation immediately around them. On one occasion, during windy weather, the opportunity was taken to observe bees entering and leaving a nest of *B. sylvarum,* the entrance of which was in the long grass on the verge of a field. Of the 33 outgoing bees observed, 12 orientated themselves, and of the 36 incoming bees observed, 15 had to search for the entrance for some time before they found it.

In other experiments colonies were moved to new sites a few yards away from the old ones, and empty nest-boxes were placed at the old sites. Although all the bees made orientation flights on leaving the new sites of their nests, and most of them eventually managed to return to them, the majority visited the old sites after their first few foraging trips before returning to the new ones. On each of their first few returns to the old sites they actually entered the empty nest-boxes which had been placed at them and, on finding them empty, left them and flew around in a perplexed manner, often for long periods, before finally departing to the new sites. Later on, after further foraging trips, they no longer tended to enter the nest-boxes at the old sites, but only to hover at their entrances for a few seconds before departing. On later visits still they would merely fly down to within a few feet of the old sites before continuing on their way to the new ones.

It was thought probable that when the old and new nest-sites were situated so close to one another returning foragers, on finding themselves near the place where their nests had been, automatically tended to go back to them by following previously established flight-routes. To test this hypothesis a colony in a nest-box was moved to a place that was still within the foraging range of the old site but a greater distance away from it (eighty yards), so there was little likelihood that bees returning to the new position of their nest would be influenced, or diverted, by any features of the environment near the original site of their nest. It was now found that, although most of the bees still visited the old site at the end of their first foraging trips, only one visited it subsequently. This result indicates, therefore, that once a forager has returned successfully to the new position of her nest she continues to do so on subsequent foraging expeditions provided she is not 'reminded' of its old position.

The orientation mechanisms normally employed by worker bumblebees are :—(i) the orientation of a bee on her first flight, (ii) the searching behaviour of a forager when she approaches her home if its surroundings have been altered during her absence, (iii) the tendency of an outgoing forager to reorientate herself when the vegetation immediately around the entrance to her nest has been disturbed. We see, therefore, that by adaptation, or extension of these orientation mechanisms, worker bumblebees are, in fact, able to adapt themselves to environmental changes much more severe than any they are likely to meet in nature.

Throughout these experiments it was very apparent that individual bees vary greatly in their learning ability, and it is as well to point out here that it is rarely safe to be dogmatic about the behaviour of any individual bee; one can only state what the majority do in given circumstances.

Apart from her visual sense, a bumblebee may also be helped to find her way back home by her sense of smell. Frison (1930) found that the scent of a nest sometimes attracts bees towards it when they are a short distance away. However, 'lost' foragers were unable to find their nest after he had displaced it by only a few feet, so that scent is unlikely to be really important in helping bumblebees to locate their nests. This subject would probably well repay further investigation.

Recent work by Blackith (1957) has revealed the interesting fact that the passage of workers in and out of a bumblebee nest does not, as one might suppose, take place entirely at random, but tends to occur in short bursts. He considers that worker bumblebees tend to be reluctant to pass through the entrances of their own nests, and has produced data which indicate that their reluctance is overcome both by the accumulation of a number of bees near the entrances of their nests and also by increase in the length of time during which they have been hesitating to pass through them. He likens their behaviour to that of cars queuing by traffic lights "in which automatic signals respond both to the numbers of vehicles and to the period for which each has been delayed". Although at moderate rates of passage the reluctance to pass through the entrances of their nests is normally overcome by the fairly rapid accumulation of individuals who are going the same way, when few bees are flying even the presence of bees going in the opposite direction may help. It would be interesting to know if the sight of bees leaving a nest helps any 'lost' foragers who are hovering about nearby to find the nest entrance.

Young queens flying from their maternal nest are even more reluctant than workers to pass through the nest entrance. Why this is so is difficult to say, but it may partially explain the observations which led Wagner (1907) to suppose that queens have greater difficulty in finding their nests than workers.

Not only do bumblebees orientate themselves to the position of their nest but they also learn the position of sources of food, and Free has noticed that bumblebees who have been collecting food from an extensive crop of flowers sometimes circle in the air as though orientating themselves before leaving for home. Manning (1956b) found that they may even orientate themselves to the positions of individual plants when visiting them for the first time, and that whether a bee does so or not depends on the distance of the plant concerned from one with whose position she is familiar. Thus, if a bee that was visiting Hound's-tongue flowers discovered a new plant that was six feet or less from a plant she already knew she never orientated before leaving it, but if the distance was greater than 6 ft. she would usually do so. Although such orientation flights were very brief, lasting only for one or two seconds, they apparently were quite sufficient to enable a bee thoroughly to establish the position of a plant, since Manning found that when he removed a plant bees sometimes returned to its site even if they had only visited it once before!

CHAPTER 15

THE ECONOMIC IMPORTANCE
OF BUMBLEBEES

Oh, for a bee's experience
Of clovers and of noon!

EMILY DICKINSON

IN 1817 Huish advocated that all bumblebees should be destroyed since honeybees must be deprived of food in proportion to the numbers of foraging bumblebees. He added, "I consider the finding of a Bumble Bees' nest as no mean treasure, for as they are like the common bee great hoarders of honey, I always rob them of their labour, and give it to my bees, who banquet on it with truly epicurean gluttony". Appreciation of the value of bumblebees has changed considerably since Huish's day; but it was not until 1859 that the attention of agriculturalists was first drawn to the valuable services bumblebees perform in pollinating important agricultural and horticultural crops. In a now famous experiment recorded in his *Origin of Species* Darwin (1859) found that 100 heads of Red Clover (*Trifolium pratense*) which were visited by bees produced 2,700 seeds whereas another 100 heads which had been protected from visiting bees produced none. The literature has grown too vast for mention to be made of more than a few observations subsequently made on the value of bumblebees as pollinators.

In a recent report published by the United States Department of Agriculture 58 crops are listed for which insect pollination is either essential or which yield more abundantly when visited by bees. Of these 22 are fruit-crops. Probably most, if not all, of these crops are at least partially dependent upon bumblebees for their pollination, but it is in connection with the pollination of red clover that bumblebees are so intimately associated (Pl. 19, p. 114). To give but a few examples, it is reported that in Denmark bumblebees are the most reliable and important pollinators of red clover; and in Finland they are practically its sole pollinators, whilst honeybees only visit it occasionally. It has been calculated that in Czechoslovakia 75 per cent—90 per cent of the bees pollinating early-flowering red clover, and 30—40 per cent of the bees pollinating late-flowering red clover—are bumblebees. Darwin (1859) and Williams (1925) have both stressed the importance of bumblebees as pollinators of red clover in this country, and recently Hawkins (1956) has made extensive observations which strongly support the opinions of these earlier workers.

The experiments of Zewakina (reported by Kurotshkin 1930) demonstrate, perhaps better than most, the ability of bumblebees to pollinate red clover flowers. Zewakina grew clover plants in storm-lantern glasses, the tops of which were covered with muslin to exclude bees. When the clover flowers were open bumblebees were caught, while collecting pollen in a clover field, and each was placed inside a glass and a note made of the number of flowers* into which each inserted her proboscis. Each bee was then removed and the clover plant kept covered until its flowering period was over, when the number of flowers which had set seed were counted. On the average 35 per cent of the flowers which had been visited on a single occasion by a bumble-bee had been fertilised.

Red clover is self-sterile, and the flowers require to be fertilised with pollen from the flowers of another red clover plant before they can set seed. The habit of bumblebees of visiting only a few flowers on a single red clover head [on the average 5 to 6 flowers per head (Free); seldom more than 8 to 10 flowers per head (Westgate and Coe 1915)] before moving on to another, would seem, therefore, to be one of the reasons why they are such efficient pollinators of this species.

Some species of bumblebees undoubtedly prefer to visit red clover flowers more than others. Observations on the kinds of

*Each red clover 'head' consists of a large number of flowers usually about 100.

BB—K

pollen collected by foragers from *B. agrorum*, *B. lucorum* and *B. sylvarum* colonies, which Free had placed beside a large field of red clover, showed that whereas the *B. agrorum* and *B. sylvarum* foragers collected loads of pollen from red clover alone, 43 per cent of the loads of pollen collected by the *B. lucorum* foragers came from other plants.

It used to be believed that honeybees seldom visited red clover flowers because they could not reach the nectar at the bottom of the long corolla tubes with their short tongues, whereas the longer-tongued bumblebees were always able to do so (see review by Butler, Free and Simpson 1956). We now know, however, that honeybees do sometimes visit red clover in considerable numbers collecting large quantities of nectar and pollen, and effectively pollinating the flowers. But the number of honeybees on a crop fluctuates considerably, no doubt partly because the nectar is often too low in the corolla tubes for them to be able to reach it, whereas the number of bumblebees tends to remain much steadier.

The value of bumblebees as pollinators of red clover is thought to be reduced by the tendency of certain short-tongued species (e.g. *B. lucorum* and *B. terrestris*) to bite holes near the bases of the corolla tubes and to obtain nectar through them without making contact with the sexual parts of the flowers and so effecting pollination (p. 110). Hawkins (1956) has recently shown that these species are certainly of less value than the long-tongued ones like *B. agrorum*, *B. hortorum*, *B. lapidarius* and *B. ruderatus*. During the flowering period Hawkins made counts, three times a week, of the number and kinds of bees present on six crops of red clover in East Hertfordshire. At intervals he also collected samples of flower-heads in order to determine the seed set. He found there were considerable variations in the numbers and kinds of pollinating insects present in the different fields, and was able to show that the yield of seed depended largely on the number of long-tongued bumblebees present, the number of short-tongued bumblebees and honeybees were of little or no consequence.

The short-tongued species, which rob the flowers of their nectar by biting holes in them, not only themselves fail to pollinate the flowers, but also enable honeybees to obtain nectar without so doing, as the latter soon learn to make use of the holes the bumblebees have bitten. Pedersen and Sørensen (1935) found that in Denmark the number of robber-honeybees on a crop was correlated with the number of robber-bumblebees present, and Stapel (1934) even suggested that extermination, or at any rate drastic suppression, of robber-bumblebees would certainly result in an increase in the value of honeybees as pollinators of red clover.   Williams (1925) found that foragers of the robber-bumblebees B. *lucorum* and B. *terrestris*, preferred to visit a Vetch (*Vicia villosa*) rather than Clover, and suggested that small areas of this former plant should be grown near clover fields so as to attract the robber-bees away from the seed-crop. However, it is generally only the nectar-gathering honeybees that act as robbers. Honeybees gathering pollen enter the flowers in the normal manner and so effect pollination. It is quite likely that the holes bitten by bumblebees enable honeybees to gather crops of honey when they would not otherwise have been able to do so; and it is even possible that such robber-honeybees attract further members of their colonies to the red clover crop to gather pollen, and so increase the degree of pollination effected.

By no means all flowers are self-sterile like red clover and possibly when bumblebees bite holes in, and steal the nectar from, flowers of self-fertile species, they may jar some of them sufficiently to pollinate them. Thus Soper (1952) has suggested that fertilisation of the Field-Bean may be brought about not only by bees who enter the flowers in the orthodox way, but also by robber-bees who, by causing movement of the flowers, may shake pollen from their anthers and on to their own stigmas. This may well be true of other self-fertile species as well.

Meidell (1944) has described one method by which robber-bumblebees sometimes effect cross-pollination. He found that whereas some bees visiting Common Cow-wheat (*Melampyrum pratense*) bite holes in the flowers and rob them of their nectar, other robber individuals actually collect pollen also. After she has robbed a flower of nectar a bee who also collects pollen places herself on the edge of the flower stretching her hind-legs across its mouth; she then vibrates her wings very rapidly, and this results in pollen being showered onto her legs. When this same bee takes up her position on the next flower her pollen-covered legs touch its projecting stigma and thus transfer to it some of the pollen she has already collected.

Another fodder crop of increasing economic importance in this country is Lucerne (*Medicago sativa*), or alfalfa as the Americans and Canadians call it. Although there is considerable evidence that honeybees are quite capable of pollinating this crop in warm, dry areas, such as those found in the southwestern parts of the U.S.A., bumblebees and other wild bees are of great importance as pollinators of it in the cooler and more humid regions of the northern parts of the U.S.A., Canada, and most of Europe (see Menke 1954; Bohart 1956). In Sweden for example it has been shown that bumblebees successfully pollinate 78 per cent of the Lucerne flowers they visit, but that visiting honeybees pollinate ess than 1 per cent (Akerberg and Lesins 1949).

Although it is mostly queen bumblebees who are available to visit fruit blossom, workers of some species are present early enough in the year to assist in the pollination of the later-flowering species and varieties. It is well known that the flowers of many different kinds of fruit-trees must receive pollen from another, compatible, variety before they will produce fruit. Other varieties, although they will produce some fruit when pollinated with their own pollen or that of other trees of the same variety, yield a larger crop, which in some cases contains larger specimens, if they are fertilised with pollen from some other, compatible variety. Bumblebees may be of greater importance than honeybees as pollinators of varieties which are to some extent self-sterile because they tend to wander more freely than honeybees from tree to tree, (Brown 1951 and Menke 1951) and thus perhaps from variety to variety.

Both Menke and Brown, who observed bumblebees visiting apple and plum blossom respectively, consider bumblebees to be more effective pollinators than honeybees, and Brown found that whereas nectar-gathering honeybees only rarely brought about the pollination of the plum flowers that they visited, bumblebees nearly always did so. He also found that the flowers of certain varieties of plum, such as 'President' and 'Jefferson', on account of the structure of their sexual organs, must be visited by large insects, such as bumblebees, for pollination to be effected. Brown thought it possible that these varieties only produce good crops when sufficient bumblebees are present. Honeybees which are seeking nectar in Cotton flowers have likewise been reported to be ineffective as pollinators, and in America bumblebees are definitely regarded as the most important pollinating agents for this crop (Thies 1953).

Even when the number of bumblebees visiting a crop is small in comparison with that of the honeybees present, it must be remembered that the pollinating value of a single bumblebee may easily equal that of two or three honeybees, since bumblebees not only work faster, but also for longer hours and in more inclement weather. Visit for visit they may also be more effective as pollinators.

At research stations where different strains or varieties of flowering crops are being selected, it is often necessary to breed them in cages or greenhouses, under conditions in which pollination can be controlled, in order to ensure that no contamination occurs. Bumblebees have been found to work well in such enclosures, and to produce good results, but their use in this connection certainly does not seem to have been exploited as much as one might have expected. Bumblebees are probably particularly suitable for pollination work in cages and similar enclosures where it is a problem to maintain honeybee colonies, and experience shows that in such conditions they work the flowers better than honeybees do and are less inclined to spend their time attempting to escape.

Lindhard (1911, 1921) was apparently the first to appreciate the value of bumblebees in plant-breeding work. He placed whole colonies of bumblebees in cages containing clover plants whose flowers he wanted pollinated, having first made sure that the individual bees were free of clover pollen by keeping them for a short time in cages containing Bird's-foot Trefoil (*Lotus corniculatus*), and obtained satisfactory results.

In his classical paper on red clover R. D. Williams (1925) of the Welsh Plant Breeding Station, Aberystwyth, reported his methods of using bumblebees. He demonstrated that when clover pollen is washed in water it loses its viability and is no longer able to effect fertilisation; he therefore washed the bumblebees he collected in tepid water, to destroy any foreign pollens on their bodies, and dried them before introducing them into cages containing red clover plants. We understand that this technique is still sometimes used today at Aberystwyth.

Minderhoud (1949), in Holland, has also used bumblebees to pollinate selected strains of Cabbage and other plants growing in small greenhouses, and he too has reported that the bumblebees did their work very well and often remained alive for a long time.

Although bumblebees are one of the most efficient pollinating insects in the world it is generally agreed that they are not numerous enough, and even in those areas where they abound in some years they are relatively scarce in others.

It is commonly supposed that the bumblebee population has declined in recent years, and it has sometimes been thought that this has resulted in a reduction in the seed produced by certain cultivated crops. This suggested decline in the bumblebee population has mostly been attributed to modern methods of intensive cultivation which tend to destroy both nests and nesting sites. The reduction in the number of hedgerows, banks, and pieces of rough ground, together with the practice of burning off the dry herbage on railway embankments and elsewhere, has no doubt helped to reduce the number of nest-sites. The increasingly extensive use of herbicides to destroy weeds in corn crops and the wild plants on roadside verges, waste ground, etc., undoubtedly reduces the sources of food on which bumblebees are partially dependent when their colonies are building-up in spring. The use of insecticides poisonous to bees, especially on early crops such as fruit, or on late crops such as certain clovers, may result in the death of the queens who visit them and so destroy the potential mothers of colonies. Even the increase in fast motor traffic on our roads has been blamed for causing casualties amongst queen bumblebees in spring. It should be remembered, however, that although the bumblebee population has probably been reduced in recent years, it is nevertheless very doubtful whether the old, supposedly high, population would have been adequate to pollinate all the flowers of our present day crops effectively.

Although it is virtually certain that there has been a decrease in the number of wild bees in Europe and N. America during the last few decades, it is very difficult to demonstrate for lack of adequate evidence. Stephen (1955) is one of the few people to produce data relating increased cultivation of the land with a decrease in the number of pollinating insects. He writes: "The production of alfalfa seed in Manitoba is most successful in the lands adjacent to uncultivated areas. The steady encroachment of agriculture into these semi-isolated areas has resulted in a progressive decrease in seed-yields until now, but a few of the formerly high yielding areas are productive . . . Within 4 to 10 years, depending on the intensity of breakaway and influence of new settlers, yields drop from 1,000 pounds to 150 pounds or so (per acre) and alfalfa seed production is no longer profitable".

Can anything be done to increase the bumblebee population? Many suggestions have been put forward, but few practical attempts have been made to do so. The most obvious suggestions have been concerned with increasing the number of nest-sites available to queens in the spring. Scarcity of nest-sites may, perhaps, not only result in some queens failing to discover suitable sites and so being unable to found nests at all in some areas, but may also, by increasing the competition for whatever sites are available, cause other queens more frequently to attempt to take possession of sites already occupied, which, as we have seen (p. 76), results in fighting and the death of one or possibly both of the queens. Queens often have to search for a long time before finding suitable places in which to nest and, consequently, their colonies may be started so late in the season that they do not have sufficient time to develop their potential complement of workers. Furthermore, the vigour of a queen may perhaps be impaired by long searching in the spring, with the result that when she does eventually found a colony she is not so prolific as she would otherwise have been. It is also possible, of course, that queens who have experienced difficulty in finding suitable nesting places eventually have to make do with sites which are not very satisfactory.

We discuss later some of the attempts that have been made to induce queens to found colonies in suitably prepared domiciles both in the field and in the laboratory (Appendix II, p. 163), and describe some of the promising results that have been achieved. Various authors have suggested that it may eventually prove to be possible to increase the bumblebee population in particular areas by inducing queens to found colonies in nest-boxes, which can then be placed where the bumblebees are required, or to induce them to nest in domiciles prepared for them near crops requiring pollination. Others, have gone so far as to envisage the development of a technique involving the controlled mating of selected queens, and the overwintering of them in captivity, with the object of producing large colonies of strains particularly suitable as pollinating agents. Such ideas seem to be divorced from reality. Even if it were possible to employ some method of inducing queens to found colonies in the laboratory with a high measure of success, it is very doubtful if it would prove an economic proposition as many of the colonies in the normal course of events fail to develop, and even the best of them only provide about 150 foragers each when they have reached their peak of strength. In any case the cost of the labour involved would be prohibitive.

The alternative of setting aside special nesting areas for bumblebees would seem to be a much more practical proposition. Plath (1934) mentions an area of ground about a quarter of an acre in extent which had been ploughed and subsequently left undisturbed. Numerous field-mice built their nests in the crevices beneath the ridges. In each subsequent year he found between 10 and 20 bumblebee colonies occupying nests which the mice had deserted, and in one year he discovered as many as eight colonies in only 10 square yards. Cumber (1953) has also reported a considerable concentration of bumblebee nests in a suitable area, in this case a certain refuse dump of 2 acres near Slough, in which, during 1947, he found 39 bumblebee nests. These nests were concentrated in certain areas, together amounting to about two-thirds of an acre, which he considered were the parts of the dump which had not been burnt over during the previous summer.

It would seem to be a simple matter for the average farmer to provide such nest-sites by deeply ploughing an odd piece of ground, and then scattering a bale or two of hay over it to provide nesting material; or, perhaps even better, to leave small areas of rough grassland undisturbed so that the grass forms thick tussocks. But much more evidence of the value of such plots in providing suitable homes for bumblebees is desirable before farmers are advised to provide them.

The lack of suitable places for young bumblebee queens to hibernate may also be a factor limiting the size of the bumblebee population in some districts, and it has been suggested that rough ground with banks that remain fairly dry throughout the winter should be made available.

Another method of increasing the bumblebee population which might be successful, would be to introduce suitable species into those parts of the world where they do not already exist. So far the only successful introductions have been of bumblebees from this country into New Zealand (see Thomson 1922), with the object of pollinating red clover which had failed to set seed there except to a very limited extent. The first successful attempts to introduce the bumblebees were made by the Canterbury Acclimatization Society in 1885 and 1886, when 93, out of a total of 442 queens shipped from England, reached New Zealand alive. The cost of importing these live queens worked out at 9/5d. each, but they soon paid for themselves since the increase in the bumblebee population during the next few years was phenomenally rapid. Bumblebees apparently became fully established throughout the country in less than 10 years and the red clover seed-crop increased considerably. New Zealand bee-keepers even became worried lest there should be insufficient nectar left for their honeybees!

However, for some unknown reason, the number of bumble-bees in New Zealand has subsequently declined; they have become scarce in areas where they were abundant, and the yield of red clover seed has fallen. The three species of bumble-bees that have become established in New Zealand, *B. latreillellus* *B. ruderatus* and *B. terrestris*, all nest underground, and Cumber has suggested that if surface-nesting species known to be efficient pollinators of red clover are introduced they might find suitable nesting sites which are not at present occupied and might, there-fore, help to swell the population again. Whilst he was in this country Cumber took the opportunity to collect queens of surface-nesting species for shipment to New Zealand, but their entry was prohibited on account of the supposed possibility of introducing the so-called 'Isle of Wight' disease of honeybees. However, our knowledge of this disease would seem to render this objection invalid, and it is to be hoped that new attempts will be made to supplement the bumblebee population of New Zealand in the near future.

There seems to be no reason why many other countries should not benefit by the introduction of bumblebees from other lands, including countries in which there are already several species, since it is, perhaps, not too much to hope that such introduced species would occupy ecological niches at present vacant. But before any alien bumblebees are released in a country, it is most important that colonies of this species should first of all be kept in enclosures in the recipient country and their foraging behaviour studied, since one never knows for certain how any insect will behave when introduced into a new country.

Both Darwin and Williams have suggested that efforts should be made to eradicate the natural enemies of bumblebees such as mice, shrews and voles. Many readers will be familiar with the passage in Darwin's *Origin of Species* in which he quotes Col. Newman as finding that the nests of bumblebees are more numerous near large towns, and for attributing this to the relatively small mouse population, due in its turn to the larger number of cats present in such areas. A German scientist, Carl Vogt, has expressed the opinion that the wealth of England was founded on her cattle which feed principally on red clover. Since, he argued, the amount of clover is dependent on bumblebees pollinating it, and a high bumblebee population is dependent on the absence of predatory mice, whose population is, in turn, dependent on the number of cats present, then the wealth of England is associated with its cat population! T. H. Huxley took this a stage further and half-humorously suggested that since old maids are fond of cats the feline population is governed by the number of old maids present! Thus one is led to the conclusion that the prosperity of England is dependent upon the number of its old maids. Nobody has, however, so far as we know, suggested increasing the numbers of old maids in our population. Although one hates to spoil a good story, it must be mentioned that nobody has been able to corroborate Col. Newman's observation that bumblebees are more numerous near towns. Furthermore, one must remember that although mice may often destroy bumblebees' nests, their own old nests provide just the places in which several species of bumblebees, like to make their homes.

Several authors have maintained that lack of spring forage prevents the establishment of many bumblebee colonies. Bohart and Knowlton (1952) have reported that the spring of 1950, which was particularly dry and cold in Fredonia, Arizona, killed many of the spring flowers and, apparently as a result, bumblebees were scarce in the district when the lucerne was in flower. They suggest that the planting of small areas with early-flowering crops, such as Hairy Vetch (*Vicia hirsuta*), would help tide bumblebees over unfavourable late spring periods. Skøvgaard (1945) of Denmark, favours the encouragement of such plants as White Deadnettle (*Lamium album*) and Yellow Archangel (*Lamium Galeobdolon*), to provide better foraging for bumblebees in spring; and Stephen (1955) has suggested that early-flowering willows should be planted in areas where lucerne is grown.

Although the provision of suitable spring flowers will undoubtedly favour an increase in the bumblebee population, the presence of abundant forage in summertime may not do so, since Cumber (1953) has pointed out that a too plentiful supply of food in the summer months might lead to larvae being fed so lavishly that their colonies would change over earlier than usual to the production of sexual brood, thus resulting in fewer workers being produced.

Another obvious suggestion is to grow the crops requiring pollination by bumblebees in those places where the latter are plentiful. It has also been proposed that such crops should be grown in small patches rather than in the large areas favoured by farmers (Richards 1953). If this were done, the limited bumblebee population would be more likely to pollinate sufficient of the flowers to guarantee a good yield of seed. Not only would there be less flowers per bee, but the available bees would be likely to forage all over such small fields, rather than being more concentrated around their edges as they are in large ones.

Lastly, suggestions have been made that the flowering of a seed-crop should be timed to coincide with the maximum bumblebee population, and this has already been practised to some extent. Williams found that in this country more bumblebees are present on red clover between the second and fourth weeks of August than at any other time, and he pointed out that growers have found by experience that crops flowering in late summer yield more seed than those in early summer. Consequently it has become an established practice in the case of some strains of red clover to mow the first crop for hay about June, and to allow the second crop, which appears about August, to run for seed. In the case of other varieties which can only be induced to flower freely once a year it is customary to delay the flowering period by grazing in early summer. Undoubtedly these methods of cultivation result in increased yields of seed partly because the flowers appear after the peak of the population of Weevils (*Apion* spp.) which attack the flower-heads has passed, but there is little doubt that the high population of bumblebees also plays an important part in increasing the seed-crop.

CHAPTER 16

BUMBLEBEES AND THEIR RELATIVES

The bee enclosed and through the amber shown,
Seems buried in the juice which was his own.

MARTIAL. *Epigrams*

ALTHOUGH some thousands of species of bees have so far been described, it is not always realised that comparatively few of them, in fact scarcely five per cent, are social in their habits. Actually, few authorities would agree on a definition of a social insect but we will follow that adopted by Imms (1947). He defined a social insect as an insect which lives in society; each society consisting of the two parents, or at least of the fecundated female, and their offspring; the two generations living to a varying extent in mutual cooperation in a common abode or shelter. Many so-called solitary bees (bees which do not live in a society) exhibit social behaviour to some extent. However, a much more highly developed form of social behaviour is exhibited by the bumblebees and, to an even greater extent, by the honeybees (Pl. 23, p. 162). In both these groups, but more particularly in the latter, a considerable degree of mutual cooperation occurs between the queen and other members of her colony, or family.

Unfortunately, the fossils of bees so far discovered are of little help in enabling us to discern the evolutionary path followed by the social bees, and it is only by studying the way of life of present day solitary, sub-social, and truly social bees that we are able to trace a probable series of evolutionary steps from the most primitive solitary bees to the most advanced social bee, the honeybee. Both Imms (1947) and Butler (1954) have, in their books in the New Naturalist series and Richards (1953) in his excellent book, already discussed the evolution of social life in insects at some length. We shall, therefore, only consider some of the ways in which the habits of bumblebees fall somewhere between those of solitary bees on the one hand, and of honeybees on the other.

Perhaps the most important difference between a solitary bee, such as one of the well-known leaf-cutting bees (*Megachilidae*) on the one hand and bumblebees and honeybees on the other, and one which explains many of the other differences also, is that a female leaf-cutting or other solitary bee never knows her off-spring at all and has died long before they reach maturity; whereas a queen bumblebee, like a queen honeybee, lives to know her mature offspring and to collaborate with them in developing their colony. In fact, as we have pointed out at the beginning of this chapter, a prerequisite of a truly social life in insects is that the life of the mother insect shall become sufficiently prolonged for her to live with her offspring. Thus we find that bumblebee queens live for three to four months after the first of their offspring have reached maturity, and queen honeybees may live as long as four to five years, outliving many generations of their worker offspring. Although a queen bumblebee may live for a little over a year, she spends seven or eight months of this time hibernating in a sheltered place, but, even so, she is certainly less well protected from the weather than a honeybee queen surrounded by a cluster of workers in a hive. A queen honeybee very seldom leaves the shelter her colony provides, but a queen bumblebee has to plough a lonely furrow in the spring, often battling against adverse weather conditions, and by the time her first young are ready to help her she already has a worn and tattered appearance.

Honeybee colonies are perennial, whereas those of bumblebees are only annual formations: furthermore, honeybee colonies become very much larger than those of bumblebees. When a colony of one of the pocket-making species of bumblebees reaches its greatest size it only consists of about 150 individuals, and even a colony of one of the more prolific of the pollen-storing species will seldom contain more than four hundred bees, but a honeybee colony will often contain tens of thousands of individuals. The queen honeybee is said to be capable of laying as many as fifteen hundred eggs daily at the height of the season, probably more than the most prolific queen bumblebee lays in her whole life!

The rate of egg-laying of both honeybee and bumblebee queens is regulated so that there are always plenty of workers to look after the brood produced. Compared with the queen bumblebee, however, the queen honeybee is little more than an egg-laying machine.

The solitary bees, bumblebees and honeybees all share the habit of obtaining their food from flowers, in the form of nectar and pollen, but the methods by which they feed their young differ widely. Female solitary bees practice what is known as mass-provisioning. Working entirely alone, a female collects sufficient food to provision each of the cells or chambers she has excavated, with a pellet of pollen moistened with honey, and on this pellet she lays a single egg. As soon as each cell has been provisioned, and an egg laid inside, it is sealed up and the female bee never looks at it again. When an egg hatches the resulting larva finds itself on a bed of food which is sufficient for its entire development. The first eggs laid by a queen bumblebee are also placed on a bed of pollen, but more pollen, as well as honey, is fed progressively to the larvae as they grow, so that frequent contact occurs between mother and offspring. It is interesting to note that in the case of some bumblebee species only the first egg cells are provided with pollen, all subsequent ones being devoid of pollen when the eggs are laid. This reminds one of the honeybees, whose queens always lay their eggs in empty cells; one in each.

Bumblebees of pocket-making species progressively feed their larvae with pollen, which is deposited from the legs of foragers directly into pockets attached to the larval groups, and it is likely that only the queen larvae are fed by the workers with pollen mixed with honey and regurgitated from their honey-stomachs. In contrast the pollen-storing species feed their larvae solely with regurgitated food. Honeybee larvae also are fed with regurgitated food but, as well as honey and pollen, they, especially queen larvae, receive a special kind of food which has a very high protein content and is produced by the pharyngeal glands of the workers. In the pocket-making species of bumblebees the larvae which come from the same egg batch remain together as a single group and compete with one another for the available pollen; any regurgitated food they receive is supplied by the adult bees through apertures temporarily made in the coating of wax which covers them. On the other hand the larvae of many of the pollen-storing species tend early in their lives to separate from their neighbours and to occupy distinct cells, each of which has a small aperture at the top which remains permanently open and through which regurgitated food is supplied. Only in their earliest stages can any competition for food take place between these larvae. Honeybee larvae are never grouped together, but each is reared from the egg in a separate open cell, and each is individually tended and fed.

It is also interesting to compare the food-gathering behaviour shown by solitary bees, bumblebees and honeybees. Whereas the female solitary bee gathers only sufficient food to provide for herself and the larvae which will hatch from the eggs she is going to lay, the amount gathered by the foragers of a bumblebee colony is dependent upon the requirements of the colony. Finally, there is no obvious limit to the amount of food that a colony of honeybees is prepared to accumulate, a characteristic which from ancient times has attracted man's attention to them.

The larva of a solitary bee develops into a perfect insect without artificial warmth of any kind; a larval bumblebee requires a certain amount of extra warmth which is generated by the adult members of its colony, but can usually withstand several hours exposure to normal daytime temperatures without coming to any serious harm. On the other hand the temperature of the brood-nest of a colony of honeybees has to be maintained constantly at a high temperature (about 32°C; (89°F.)) if the brood is to develop normally.

Both bumblebees and honeybees possess glands capable of secreting the wax which they use for building their combs, but the solitary bees do not produce or use wax in this way. However, whereas all the cells of a honeybee comb are made of wax, bumblebees will use old cocoons, as well as specially prepared

---

Plate 21 (opposite). FORAGING BUMBLEBEES. C.
above. B. *pratorum* worker gathering pollen and nectar from a Dianthus flower. Note the specks of pollen on her hairy body as well as in her pollen-basket (x 1·8)
below. B. *agrorum* queen collecting nectar from a Dandelion (x 1·6)

Plate 21

Plate 22

waxen cells, in which to store food. Although bumblebees are economical with wax and remove it from around pupal cocoons and add it to expanding larval cells and make additional honey-pots with it, the honeybees are considerably more economical in the use of wax since they employ the same cells over and over again for raising one generation of brood after another. Thus the wax produced by bygone generations of workers continues to be used by their successors for many years.

The eggs laid by a female solitary bee produce either perfect males or perfect females. Such males and females mate and the latter eventually make nests of their own. In the case of the social bumblebees and honeybees, however, males and two kinds of females are produced. Females of one kind are fully developed sexually and are known as queens, and the sexual organs of the other kind remain undeveloped and they are known as workers. Since only the queens are able to produce further females, the workers are concerned almost exclusively with such matters as the building and defending of the comb, and with obtaining food and caring for the brood. Whether or not a female bumblebee larva becomes a queen or worker seems to depend on its food-supply. If a larva receives ample food it develops into a queen, but if it is partially starved it becomes a worker. It is possible that the worker caste may have originated because the egg-laying females (queens) became more prolific and in consequence more larvae were produced than could be supplied with sufficient food for full development, with the result that small, sexually un-developed, females, eventually emerged and functioned as workers. Alternatively, of course, the egg output of the queens may have remained constant but, for one reason or another, they may have become unable to provide their larvae with sufficient food for them to develop into queens.

Workers of the pocket-making species of bumblebees show all gradations of size up to that of queens, but there is a sharp demarcation in size between workers and queens of certain pollen-storing species although workers and queens still vary in size among themselves. Finally, there is hardly any variation at all in the size of honeybee workers, which are much smaller than the queen. Whereas in the case of both the pocket-making species, and the pollen-storing species, of bumblebees it is the quantity of food that the female larvae receive which determines their destiny, the differentiation between worker and queen honeybees appears to be partially governed by a hormone present in the larval food, although future queen larvae do in fact consume considerably more food than larvae from which workers are derived.

Apart from size, a bumblebee queen is similar in physical appearance to her workers, and most of the differences between them are associated with the ability of the former to mate, build up her fat-bodies and to hibernate. She can perform all the duties carried out by workers and, in fact, has to do so when founding her colony. Only when her offspring are old enough to go foraging regularly does she cease to collect food herself and devote her attention exclusively to household duties. Even so she carries out many tasks such as building the egg-cells, incubating, and probably feeding, the brood, as well as laying eggs. A queen honeybee on the other hand performs no other duties than egg-laying, and indeed is physically incapable of so doing, since during the course of time she has become structurally modified so that she no longer possesses the necessary equipment in the shape of pollen-baskets, wax-glands and pharyngeal glands. She has a shorter tongue and a sting that differs in shape from those of workers.

Male honeybees have also become physically more specialised than male bumblebees, and, unlike the latter, are apparently unable to feed themselves from flowers; furthermore they return each night to the shelter of their hives. Worker honeybees also seem more dependent on a social way of life than do worker bumblebees. An individual worker bumblebee kept in isolation will sometimes even build a honeypot and an egg-cell in which she lays eggs—she will, in fact, behave like a queen—but, of course, as her eggs are unfertilised, only males would be produced from her brood.

Queens and males are produced towards the end of the life of a bumblebee colony, and their production is soon followed by dissolution of the colony, only the young queens surviving the winter to found new colonies the next year (Pl. 22, p. 147). Honeybee colonies are perennial and have evolved a special method of colony reproduction and dispersal known as swarming, which entails the production of young queens shortly before the swarm departs. Indeed a queen honeybee is certainly not fitted to found a colony on her own.

Not only does caste differentiation result in a division of labour between the queen and her workers, but there is also a division of labour between the workers themselves. In the case of both bumblebee and honeybee colonies the age of an individual worker appears to determine to some extent when she will give up purely household duties and become a forager, but the proportion of her life that a bumblebee worker spends either as a household bee or as a forager is to some extent predetermined by her size. The particular task which a honeybee worker is fitted to perform at any one time is also governed by the physiological condition of certain of her glands, but we have little evidence of how far, if at all, this is true of bumblebees. The division of labour among both worker bumblebees and worker honeybees is not rigid but is adaptable to meet the current requirements of their colonies, so that efficient use is made of the labour force available.

Animals who lead solitary lives are frequently hostile to other members of their own species, especially to those of the same sex as themselves. How is it that the members of a family of social bees not only tolerate each other but actually cooperate together for the common good, obtaining food for, and defending, not only themselves but their colony as a whole? Undoubtedly one factor of importance in their mutual tolerance is that they are all reared in the same nest and come to acquire a common odour. Another, and perhaps the most important of all, is that usually only one of the female bees present has developed ovaries and lays eggs to any great extent. If this were not so too much brood might be produced and the continued existence of the colony jeopardised. When more than one egg-laying individual is present in a bumblebee colony aggressiveness develops between them and the usual state of peaceful coexistence disappears (See Chapter 7, p. 52).

In bumblebee colonies the inhibition of the reproductive tendencies of workers may be largely psychological, and a queen bumblebee seems to reduce the tendency of her workers to lay eggs by actively dominating them, the workers being able to recognise her by her characteristic scent. In contrast, a queen honeybee produces on the surface of her body a substance (queen substance) which the workers obtain by licking it. Frequent transfer of food directly from one worker to another occurs in a honeybee colony and in this 'queen substance' is constantly passed, so that all the members of the colony remain 'aware' of the presence of their queen(Butler 1954). This inhibits queen rearing by the workers and also prevents their ovaries from developing. It may be that this queen substance has developed from the distinctive scent produced by the queen, or other dominant individual, present in communities of less advanced social insects, such as the bumblebee.

Normally no direct transfer of food takes place between one bumblebee and another, but very occasionally when a worker bumblebee attacks another the individual attacked will regurgitate a drop of food between her open mandibles and offers it to her attacker. Similarly when a honeybee worker strays to the entrance of the hive of another colony by mistake, and is intercepted and examined by the guard-bees, she frequently offers them a drop of regurgitated food. Perhaps the transference of food between worker honeybees, which plays such an important part in their social organisation, has evolved from the habit of an attacked bee offering food to her aggressor, as bumblebees as well as honeybees, sometimes do.

Thus, we find that the bumblebees with their interesting habits enable us to trace how some of the behaviour of their relatives the honeybees, together with their much larger and more advanced societies, may have arisen.

THE COLLECTION AND STUDY
OF BUMBLEBEE COLONIES

Go to the bee, thou poet, consider her ways and be wise.

BERNARD SHAW. *Man and Superman*

THE most promising places in which to search for bumblebees'
nests are rough uncultivated verges and banks, and patches
of waste ground that have been left undisturbed for some years.
Areas where the grass is tussocky provide particularly good
hunting grounds for surface-nesting species.

Nests are especially difficult to locate at the beginning of the
season when colonies are still small and few bees are flying from
them, but later in the season when colonies have grown and
contain more flying bees the nests become easier to find. The
onset of a shower of rain causes many of the foraging bumblebees
to return home and, for a short while, this makes it much easier
to spot the whereabouts of the entrance of a nest as the bees
rush to it.

Sladen gives the following advice:—"To discover the nests
it is best to walk slowly along the foot of the bank or the outside
of the wood, stopping at times, and all the while keeping one's
eyes resting on a spot about twenty yards ahead on the bank or
in the wood, ready to follow with the eye, if not on foot, every
humble-bee that can be seen or heard . . . If we are in East
Kent, though other parts of the country can hardly differ much
in this respect, we shall be rewarded in a few minutes by the
sight of a humble-bee either leaving or entering its nest".

Any disturbance to the vegetation and other landmarks
around a nest causes its foragers to experience difficulty in

finding the entrance on their return home, and, in their searches, they often give away its approximate position. Windy weather often disturbs the vegetation around a nest's entrance and has this effect, and Cumber found it helpful when searching for nests to drag a leafy branch across likely nesting areas in order to achieve the same result. When hayfields are cut the whereabouts of any nests are similarly revealed by the bees hovering and circling in the air nearby.

We have found that the most certain, and definitely the easiest, method of procuring nests is to advertise for them in a local newspaper, although of course, one loses the satisfaction of finding them for oneself. Towards the middle and end of the summer advertising brings a large number of responses from householders who in most cases are only too glad to find somebody willing to remove nests. Many such nests are found in, or under, paving stones, garden sheds, hen-houses, old sacking and upholstery, heaps of lawn-mowings, piles of bricks and wood, and all sorts of by-products of human civilisation; and the collector is soon made aware of how adaptable bumblebees are in their nesting habits. On two occasions we have been notified of nests that were situated somewhere beneath tombstones but, needless to say, decided to let them remain where they were. It is also a good idea to get in touch with the local pest control officer, the police, and the county beekeeping instructor, since they are sometimes called upon to destroy colonies whose members are being a nuisance.

The most satisfying method of all of obtaining colonies is to induce queens to start them in the laboratory, or in specially prepared domiciles out-of-doors, but more will be said about this in Appendix II, p. 163.

Having discovered a colony, the next thing to do is to take it safely back home. For this purpose, the following equipment will be found most useful; a box, complete with lid, in which to place the comb—the nest-box to be described shortly will do ideally; a bag or box in which to place the nesting material; a trowel; up to a dozen jars with perforated lids (1 lb. honey jars are excellent); a pair of forceps; some rag or cotton wool and a bottle of chloroform; an electric torch, although not essential, will sometimes be found useful. One rarely knows in advance what species one is likely to be dealing with and, since underground nesting species such as *B. lucorum* and *B. terrestris* can be very resentful when disturbed, it is always a good idea to carry a veil, such as beekeepers use.

The best time to collect a nest located on the surface of the ground is either at the beginning or at the end of the day, when most of the bees will be at home, and it is comparatively simple to scoop up the whole nest, bees and all, put it into a box, and close the lid before any of the inhabitants have had time to fly away. If the nest proves difficult to remove from its surroundings, it is best to wrap one's veil or a piece of fine netting around its top and sides, so that any bees which try to take flight while it is being freed are effectively trapped. Another good idea is to invert a small, empty box or other container over the nest, and to force a metal plate through the vegetation beneath it, so that the nest is enclosed in the box.

Often, however, it is only convenient to collect colonies during daytime when a proportion of their members will be out foraging. Also, unless one works at night by torchlight, which is rather tedious, it is impossible to collect colonies that are situated underground and in other relatively inaccessible places without a large number of bees flying out of them.

If some of the members of a surface-nesting colony are flying, it is best to start gradually unravelling the nesting material and, as each bee appears, to grab her with the forceps and put her into a jar. The bees should be grasped by their wings or legs, preferably the hind-legs as these are the strongest; such treatment seems to do the bees no harm. If one has no forceps one can pick up the bees by firmly grasping their wings, as close to their bodies as possible, between a finger and thumb. If this is done carefully they are unable to sting. The tendency of bumblebees to roll over onto their backs ready to sting any intruder when their nest is disturbed (Pl. 14a, p. 67) makes this method of collection difficult, but facilitates their collection when forceps are used.

If it is intended to put several bees into one jar, it is best to take the lid off temporarily and to keep the jar covered for the time being with a piece of stiff card or wood which can be slid to one side just sufficiently to allow another bee to be inserted.

Immediately before putting in another bee give the jar a sharp shake so that the bees already in it are thrown to the bottom. Sheets of glass painted black so that the light cannot get through them are excellent for covering the mouths of the jars. Clear glass is not satisfactory as a lid since the bees tend to fly up against it and thus make it much more difficult to insert a fresh captive without losing some of those already present.

It is worth mentioning that when trapped in a jar bees are liable to regurgitate the contents of their honey-stomachs and to defaecate, and consequently may become very moist and sticky. To avoid this trouble it is a good idea to put some shreds of tissue or blotting paper in the jars to absorb the moisture. Flowers or pieces of grass placed in the jars are also useful as they help to provide a foothold for the bees. The jars should always be perfectly dry before use and one should never put more than 15 bees into one jar. As soon as a jar contains its complement of bees the perforated lid should be replaced and the jar put into a dark place, since darkness helps to calm the bees. The jars containing bees must always be kept in the shade, since, if they are exposed to the direct rays of the sun, the atmosphere inside them quickly becomes very hot, causing the deaths of the captives.

A little while after starting to collect a surface nest one finds that one has captured most of the adult bees that have run out from it, and the comb itself will have become exposed. At this stage the most important thing to do is to find the queen. She will most likely be hiding somewhere in the comb or nesting material, although, of course, one should have been looking out for her all the time and may perhaps have caught her already. As she is by far the most important member of the colony it is wise to make a point of placing her in a jar by herself, so that there is no risk of her becoming damaged during any excitement or scuffling on the part of the workers. The comb will probably also contain many small workers who are reluctant to fly, as well as newly emerged bees who are not yet strong enough to do so. When these have been captured the comb should be lifted out and placed in a box that has previously been prepared for it. This operation must be performed with great care, since the delicate cells are easily crushed and parts of the comb may readily break away. To help to protect the comb the collecting box should be lined with grass or cotton-wool. The nesting material should now be thoroughly searched, as one nearly always finds that several bees have buried themselves in it in their efforts to escape.

It is a good plan after taking the comb and catching the queen and as many workers as possible, to remove all one's equipment about ten yards away from the site and stand well back. Those foragers who have returned and are hovering in the air, together with any bees who have escaped from the nest, will soon alight on the nesting material that enclosed their comb, although at first they show a great deal of hesitation. A visit to the site every few minutes is bound to result in the collection of additional members of the colony. However, it is not worth waiting to collect returning foragers for more than an hour, since very few remain away from home for longer than this. If possible one should leave some of the nesting material on the site and come back, after flying has ceased for the day, to capture any additional bees who may have settled on it. If, however, one is able to return to the site at this time of day, the following much more simple and effective method should be used. At the first visit, when many bees are still flying, simply lift up the nest and, having transferred it to an open box, place it on the site it previously occupied. Foragers soon find the nest on their return and enter it, so that when the collector comes back at dusk all he has to do is to place the lid on the box and carry it home!

Underground colonies are usually not so easy to collect, and their capture often entails tedious and sometimes fruitless digging. The most difficult part of the operation is to avoid losing track of the entrance tunnel while digging down to the nest, and it is a good idea to insert a length of rubber tubing, or a pliable willow wand, into the tunnel, to make it easier to follow. Even when this has been done it is easy to go astray, and if this happens it is best to pack up for the day and visit the site again a day or two later, when the bees may have dug another entrance tunnel.

In the case of *B. lucorum* and *B. terrestris* colonies it is important to try to capture the bees as they rush up the entrance tunnel from the nest, especially the first few, as these are likely to be guards and are usually the most pugnacious. Should the bees become too ferocious they may be quietened by stuffing rag or cotton-wool soaked with chloroform into the tunnel, although a cylinder containing nitrous oxide (laughing gas), or carbon dioxide, is more useful for this purpose, since a length of rubber tubing fitted to the nozzle of the cylinder can be inserted right down the tunnel, and the amount of gas given can be regulated as required. During the final stages of the operation care must be taken in removing the earth from around the comb. However, the loud commotion set up by the occupants gives ample warning when one gets near the nest itself.

Having collected a colony, the comb and bees should be placed together again as soon as possible. Any box of convenient size will do as a home for the colony; cigar-boxes are quite suitable for small colonies, while shallow biscuit tins of standard size do admirably for larger ones. The sort of nest-box we have found most useful is shown in Fig. 2, p. 157. It consists of two intercommunicating compartments, one serving to hold the nest, the other acting as an outer chamber or vestibule, both being covered with sheets of glass. The idea of having a vestibule was first thought of by Sladen, and, although not essential, it has been found to be a most useful place in which to put food for collection by the bees, and also provides a suitable place for them to excrete and so prevents fouling of the nest-compartment. The floor of the vestibule should be covered with corrugated cardboard, or several layers of blotting paper, which can be changed periodically. The holes bored in the side of the nest-box not only serve as ventilators but it is also possible to reach the various parts of the comb through them with the minimum of disturbance to the bees. Adequate ventilation must always be given, and it is a good idea to provide rather more than one thinks is necessary.

As the comb grows in size it is possible to fit extra sections on top of the nest-box to accommodate it. However, a bumble-bee comb is naturally dome-shaped, and if the bees are compelled by the shape of their home to build it upwards rather than outwards the amount of comb that can be observed is limited. If a comb grows outward sufficiently to fill the floor area of the nest-box, it is best to transfer it to a larger box. This difficulty may, of course, also be overcome by constructing nest-boxes which can be expanded by moving their walls outwards.

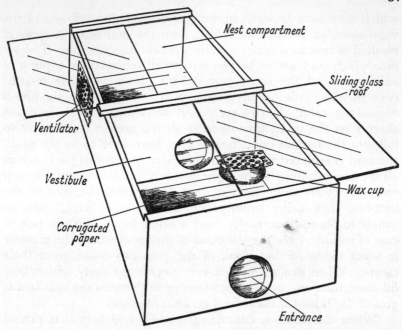

Nest compartment

Sliding glass roof

Ventilator

Vestibule

Wax cup

Corrugated paper

Entrance

FIG 2

A nest box which will be found suitable for housing a bumblebee colony

The amount of nesting material that should be placed in a nest-box depends upon the circumstances. There should always be enough to cover the base of the comb, but if too much is given the bees will hide the comb completely from view. In order to avoid introducing any parasites (see Chapter 10, p. 80), it is best not to use the original nesting material: grass or moss that has previously been dried will do very well instead, and is readily acceptable to the bees. Materials such as cotton-wool should not be used, as the bees seem to have difficulty in manipulating it and may become entangled in it.

The comb should be gently lowered into the nest-box prepared for it. If there is not much food present it is as well to fill a few of the cells with sugar syrup. The queen is now introduced and she often makes her way hastily into the midst of the comb. The worker bees can be removed one at a time from the jars in which they were brought home and pushed through one of the ventilators, or the entrance hole, into the nest-box. A quicker method is first to transfer all the workers into one jar. The jar into which they are to be put has its lid replaced by a piece of stiff card, and the other jars, which also have their mouths covered with cards, are inverted over it one at a time; the pieces of card separating the two are pulled away and the jars bumped sharply on the table, thus causing all the bees in the top jar to fall into the bottom one; before they have time to fly up again the card is replaced over the bottom jar. When this jar contains all the bees it is inverted over the nest-box and its contents thrown onto the comb with one vigorous shake, the glass roof of the nest-box then being rapidly slid back into position. This is simple to do and one rarely loses a single bee, although, just in case of trouble, close the windows of the room where the transfer is being made so that none of the bees can make good their escape. When dealing with a very populous colony whose bees fill more than one jar the transference of them to the nest-box is greatly facilitated if they are first anaesthetised.

When the nest-box contains the comb and bees it is placed on a bench or shelf, beside an outer wall if in a hut or similar building, or window if in a room. A hole an inch in diameter is bored through the wall of the hut, or through the window-frame or the glass of the window itself, and provides ample communication for the bees between the nest-box and the outside world. The entrance of the nest-box can be pushed right up against this hole, but it is more convenient, when one wishes to watch the bees going in and out, if a glass tube through which they can pass is interposed between the nest-box and the window. This tube can be anything up to about two feet long, and a thin layer of sand placed in it provides the bees with a secure foothold.

The bees should not be allowed to fly until several hours after they are introduced into their nest-box, so that they may settle down in their new home. At first, it is best to keep the glass roof of the nest-box covered with some dark material to exclude the light so that the workers can more readily find the exit, otherwise they are apt to spend their time battering themselves against the glass trying to get out. After a few days, however, this covering can be removed so that the activities of the bees can be observed. They soon grow accustomed to the light and cease to take any notice of it, but rays of direct sunlight on the nest-box should, of course, be avoided as the air inside it would tend to become too hot.

To facilitate the orientation of the bees to their new surroundings a coloured disc should be placed near to the entrance hole on the outside of the building, and it helps returning bees to alight if a small platform is provided for them just beneath the entrance. It is as well to keep the windows near the nest closed as otherwise erring foragers may find their way into the room from time to time, especially if they are driven home in haste by a shower of rain.

For experimental purposes it is sometimes necessary to have colonies one is watching located in the field. In such cases the observer must remain hidden from the flying bees, otherwise they hesitate to return home. The following simple method of achieving this has been found to be most effective:—the observer sits behind a vertical wooden screen about 6 ft. high and 6 ft. long. On the same side of the screen as the observer, and about 3 ft. from the ground, a wooden platform is fixed and the nest-box is placed on this platform with a glass entrance tunnel connecting it to the front of the screen. When the colony is not being observed the nest-box should be covered with an inverted tin box, or a piece of some other waterproof material, to keep it dry.

There is one further point which should be mentioned. If the colony is to be kept within foraging distance of where it was originally collected, some of the foragers may return to the old site, but many of them will, nevertheless, eventually manage to find their way back to their new home again (see Chapter 14, p. 126).

During inclement weather when the bees cannot fly, although they will brave all but the very worst conditions, it is as well to provide them with food in the nest. Feeding should be discontinued as soon as conditions become favourable so that the bees are encouraged to forage for themselves. Sugar syrup, made by dissolving one part of sugar in one part of water (both by weight), will be found suitable for this purpose. If it is made too concentrated the sugar tends to crystallize out. The syrup may be placed in any small receptacle, which should, however, be covered with a piece of wire-gauze through which the bees can feed without running any risk of falling in. A small wax cup for holding the syrup can be made quite simply by dipping the bottom of a wet specimen tube into a tin containing melted wax. Within a minute or two the wax cup thus formed has set hard enough to be slipped off the end of the tube. Bumblebees will also take syrup readily from a gravity feeder which consists of a vertical glass tube with one small opening at its lower end. Such tubes are filled with syrup and placed vertically with their mouths downwards. Every three or four days all the feeders should be washed out and filled with fresh syrup, since syrup of the concentration recommended soon ferments. Bumblebee colonies rarely become short of pollen, but, should this occur, they may be provided with pollen taken from the combs of honeybee colonies.

During experimental work it is often necessary to be able to recognise individual bees, and this is achieved by marking them with paints. Even if it is not required for experimental work a bumblebee colony whose bees are all distinctively marked becomes particularly interesting since the activities of individuals can be followed with ease. It is not possible to mark bumblebees as neatly as honeybees, on account of the more hairy covering of their bodies, but their large size, which enables larger marks to be used, makes up for this disadvantage. Quick-drying cellulose paints made up with an acetone solvent are most satisfactory for this purpose, and should be thinned to a fairly fluid consistency before application.

Marks made on the thorax are most easily seen. When marking a bee, it is best to hold her down on a flat surface with a pair of forceps so that the wings are kept well out of the way (Pl. 15b, p. 82). It is a great help when marking bees, and almost essential if individually distinctive marks are being applied, to anaesthetize the bees. Bumblebees are readily anaesthetized with any of the common anaesthetics; of these, chloroform is quite satisfactory and probably the most readily available, although on account of their ease of use, cylinders of nitrous oxide or carbon dioxide should be purchased by anybody likely to have to mark many bees. When using chloroform one must take care that none of the liquid comes into contact with the bees. A wad of cotton-wool soaked in chloroform is placed in the bottom of a tube or jar and covered by a layer of wire-gauze onto which the bumblebee to be anaesthetised is dropped. Since a bumblebee can easily be given an overdose of chloroform from which she never recovers she should be removed from the jar while still moving her limbs.

When choosing the marks to be put on a bee the fact that parts of them may flake off in time must be taken into consideration. For this reason combinations of different coloured spots are not very satisfactory unless there is always a fixed number of them per bee, or unless they are arranged in definite positions on the thorax, as otherwise one can never be sure whether one or more of them has become erased. We have found that many of the letters of the alphabet are very suitable as distinctive marks and, by taking care in choosing them, it is nearly always possible to recognise what the letter originally was even though a part of it may have become rubbed off. If a colony contains large numbers of bees to be distinctively marked, the letters can be orientated in different directions relative to the bees' bodies, and different colours can be used as well. All sorts of symbols can, of course, be devised, but there is a danger that unless they mean something definite to the observer, (as letters of the alphabet obviously do), they are liable to be confused with one another, especially at times when rapid identification is necessary. If it is only necessary to recognise bees as members of parti-cular colonies, all that is required is that each member of the same colony shall be marked with a spot of paint of the same colour.

In various types of experiment that have been carried out on bumblebees the relative sizes of the bees of a colony have had to be ascertained. This is done either by weighing them indivi-dually, or by measuring the length of some anatomical feature of their bodies, such as the length of a wing, which increases proportionately with general body-size.

When weighing bees it should be borne in mind that some bees will undoubtedly have more food in their honey-stomachs, and more faeces in their recta than others. Since this may apply to foragers especially, it is best to confine all the members of a colony in their nests for several hours before weighing them, so that any difference between the weights of foragers and household bees that are associated with the contents of their alimentary canals will be minimized.

The hints given above will, we hope, prove of value and help would-be students of bumblebees to avoid many of the pitfalls into which one inevitably stumbles when first one tries to collect and keep colonies of these interesting insects.

Plate 23 (opposite) A HONEYBEE COLONY IN THE WILD
A Honeybee colony, unlike those of British bumblebees and social wasps, is perennial and as many as 20,000-30,000 workers survive the winter with their queen. This colony has built its combs in a hollow tree (x 1·7)

Plate 24

STARTING COLONIES IN CAPTIVITY

My banks they are furnish'd with bees,
Whose murmur invites one to sleep.
WILLIAM SHENSTONE. *A Pastoral Ballad*

THE initial stages of the development of a bumblebee colony, from the time when the queen lays her first eggs until her earliest fluffy offspring make their appearance are among the most interesting of all to observe. Unfortunately, however, one does not often come across a colony in the field until it is well established, and the numerous workers flying in and out of it attract one's attention. Various methods have been devised to induce queens to found colonies in the laboratory or in prepared sites in the field, and it has been by making use of these methods that we have gained much of our knowledge of the early stages of a bumblebee colony. Several workers have spent a good deal of time attempting to develop a really efficient method of inducing queens to found their colonies either in captivity, or in specially prepared domiciles out-of-doors, so that they can be made available in those areas where the services of bumblebees as pollinating agents for red clover and other seed-crops are particularly desirable.

The method that has been used to induce bumblebee queens

Plate 24 (opposite). COLONY FOUNDING IN CAPTIVITY
Normally queen bumblebees are antagonistic to one another and each queen founds her colony entirely on her own; but, in captivity, they can sometimes be induced to cooperate together.
above. Two *B. terrestris* queens incubating side by side (x 1·9)
below. *B. agrorum* queen (left hand side) is helping a *B. terrestris* queen even after the first of the latter's workers have emerged (x 1·5)
BB—M

to found their colonies in selected places in the field is, in general, similar to that of providing birds with boxes in which to nest, with the important difference that whereas birds collect their own nesting material bumblebee queens do not and the domiciles for them must contain suitable materials. As early as 1887 Haviland recorded that "The great John Hunt in springtime made places for the humblebees well provided with moss and

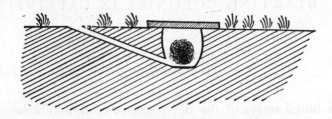

FIG 3

Cross section of a bumblebee domicile. It consists simply of a hole dug in the ground, in which is placed the nesting material, connecting with the exterior through a narrow tunnel

covered with moveable slabs", and that several of them were occupied by queen bumblebees; but it was Sladen (1912) who made the first extensive attempts to attract queens to artificial domiciles.

Anybody reading Sladen's fascinating account of his work cannot but be impressed by the infinite care he took in trying to provide the conditions that he thought would be most attractive to searching queens. His early type of domicile consisted of a hole, dug in the ground to the depth of about a foot, which contained nesting material. The top of the hole was covered with a metal plate. An entrance tunnel, made by driving an iron rod into the ground, connected this hole with the outside world. Its exit was made about 18 inches from the edge of the hole, and the tunnel sloped at such an angle that it entered the nest-cavity near the bottom. The vegetation was plucked short around the entrance so that it might more easily be seen by queens who were searching for nesting places. Later Sladen used what he called a 'tin domicile'. A tin cylinder covered with a lid was placed inside the hole and a small ball of nesting material, about four inches in diameter, was placed on the soil at the bottom of it; the tunnel leading to the nest was made in the same way as before. He tried a variety of nesting materials including dead grass, soft moss, and unravelled rope cut to half-inch lengths. He even went so far as to cut half rotted grass into lengths of about two inches, "carefully picking out the stalks and heads". He found that this last material was the most suitable.

Thirty-three out of a total of 139 domiciles of the earlier type, and 17 out of 53 of the later type, were occupied by queens, so that altogether 26 per cent of his domiciles became occupied. However, one gathers that many of the domiciles became damp and unserviceable, and that a number of those occupied by queens were later abandoned by them because of the intrusion of centipedes, millipedes, slugs, bettles, ants, mice and shrews.

An American, Frison (1926b), also started experimenting with similar domiciles in 1915. His original type of domicile consisted of a tin fitted with a spout from the base to serve as an entrance tunnel, the whole thing being rather like a watering-can except that it had no handle and was fitted with a lid. He buried these domiciles so that both the lid and the end of the spout were level with the surface of the ground. Later, improved models were fitted with fine copper-gauze bottoms, in place of the previous solid ones, so as to provide drainage for the water that accumulated inside. Later he also employed small rectangular wooden boxes, with metal tubing, or lengths of rubber hosepipe, as entrance tunnels. Each domicile was furnished with a field-mouse's nest. Seventeen out of 36 of Frison's domiciles (47 per cent) were occupied by queens, but in only 6 cases did the colonies reach maturity. However, a high mortality rate is probably quite usual; for instance, of 80 colonies of *B. agrorum* which Cumber (1953) kept under observation, 25 died out prematurely and only 23 produced any queens.

Frison found that the siting of domiciles is most important in determining whether or not they will attract queens. Queens seeking places in which to start their nests are exceedingly 'inquisitive', and if domiciles are located near objects which stand out from their surroundings, and to which queens are attracted, such as fence-posts, rocks, logs, and trees, there is a much greater chance of them being discovered.

Frison was more successful with his domiciles than Sladen; it is possible that this was partly because they may have been better designed, but may also have been partly due to the provision of a mouse's nest in each. Free used Sladen-type domiciles and obtained greater success when he put some nesting material of a mouse in them than when he used anything else. It seems probable that it is the fine soft texture into which mice work their nesting materials that makes it so acceptable to searching queens. The smell of a mouse's nest may also attract queens, but no success was achieved when Free added a few crystals of acetamide, a chemical which in its usual commercial form smells to man like mice, to nest-material placed in domiciles.

Attempts have also been made to induce queens to adopt particular domiciles by confining them inside them for several hours, or by putting anaesthetized queens into them but leaving their entrances open. Although, when they left them, many of the queens obviously studied the positions of the entrances to the domiciles in which they had been placed, and a few returned again, none remained to start her colony. Why this was so we do not know.

The type of domicile so far discussed appears to attract almost exclusively queens of those species who usually make their homes partly or wholly beneath the ground. However, early in his work Sladen placed 33 balls of grass on the surface of the ground and in 2 of them queens (1 *B. agrorum* and 1 *B. hortorum*) started nests. These two species are among the best pollinators of red clover and if a simple form of surface domicile could be devised which would readily attract their queens it might well prove to be of importance. With this end in view, in the spring of 1952, Free set out 92 surface domiciles, 19 of which merely consisted of dry lawn-mowings made into balls and placed under thick grass-tufts, and 73 of balls of dry grass or shredded cellulose-wadding placed under flower-pots, boxes and roofs of beehives. Unfortunately only 6 queens (4 *B. agrorum* and 2 *B. helferanus*), all of surface-nesting species, established their homes in them.

Much more promising results have been reported from America by Fye and Medler (1954b). Most of their domiciles consisted of wooden boxes, and to overcome the difficulty of providing the right sort of nesting material they used a simple but ingenious idea to induce mice to nest before the bumblebee queens come along. They partly filled their boxes with flax straw, put a handful of grain in each to attract the mice, and distributed them around the countryside in August and September. By the following spring 112 out of 130 of their boxes contained mouse-nests. The mice were driven from the boxes and their re-entry was prevented by reducing the size of the entrance-holes. The domiciles were then left to attract searching bumblebee queens, and 52 of them were occupied. It is encouraging to note that Fye and Medler regard 4 of the 5 species of queens that their domiciles attracted as exceptionally good pollinators of Red Clover and other legumes. Unfortunately, 37 of their domiciles were overrun by ants, but they have since found an effective way of controlling these insects so it is to be hoped that they may have even more success in the future.

Another method of inducing queens to occupy domiciles has recently been reported by Stein (1956b). He liberated several queens in a large cage in which he had placed a liberal supply of pollen and honey together with a number of boxes containing straw or grass. Some of the queens discovered these boxes and started their nests in them.

We may conclude that domiciles placed out-of-doors to attract searching queens should provide darkness, shelter from the elements (especially damp) and protection from vermin, and should be located in places where queens are likely to search, especially near prominent landmarks. They should possess conspicuous entrances and should contain fine nesting material, that forming mouse-nests apparently being ideal.

It should be realised that the results obtained with any sort of outside domicile depend a great deal on the numbers of searching queens that are about and, unfortunately, their numbers fluctuate enormously from year to year. However, even in a poor year one can usually capture enough queens to get a number of colonies started in confinement indoors. Although all the successful methods so far devised for inducing queens to nest in confinement are too tedious and time-consuming to be of economic value in securing colonies for pollination, they are well worth reviewing, both for their own sake, and because they do form a practical method of obtaining colonies and watching their development throughout the season.

A number of early workers e.g. Hoffer (1882), Sladen (1912), Lindhard (1912), Plath (1923b) and Frison (1918 and 1927b), succeeded in getting colonies started by confining queens in specially prepared nest-boxes in the laboratory, but as Frison was the only worker to achieve any notable degree of success we will confine our discussion to his methods.

Frison's nest-boxes were divided into two intercommunicating compartments, one of which was covered with a sheet of glass and acted as the 'outside world' in which a small cup containing diluted honey was placed. The other compartment formed the nest-chamber and was lined throughout with 4 or 5 layers of muslin coated with wax. He provided an artificial wax honey-pot, made to match as nearly as possible the honeypot which a nesting queen constructs for herself, and also a ball of pollen about the size of a cherry-stone. In other words he provided everything he could to encourage the queen to settle down and found a colony—in fact he furnished the compartments.

He did not place the queens he had caught into nest-boxes straight away but first confined them in large glass aquarium jars, since he thought that exercise might be essential for them at this stage. Ample food was provided in the jars and the queens were kept there until they became 'broody'. A broody queen behaves in a very characteristic manner, which is associated with her physiological condition. She produces wax and will try to incubate lumps of pollen, artificial honeypots or any other small objects, and, when disturbed, she buzzes excitedly and moves around the object she has been incubating in an agitated way. As soon as a queen became broody Frison put her into one of his artificial nests. In most cases two queens were placed together in each nest-box, but sometimes only a single queen was confined in a box. Using this technique in 1919 and 1920 he succeeded in getting eggs laid in 22 out of 31 nest-boxes (over 70 per cent) but in only 10 cases were the first batch of larvae reared successfully.

No further advances in technique for inducing queens to found colonies in captivity were made known until Hasselrot (1952) of Sweden published the results of his preliminary work.

He captured queens early in the spring and kept them in match-boxes in a refrigerator until "the proper time for nesting seemed to have come". The queens were then confined individually in nest-boxes, each of which consisted of two intercommunicating compartments, the smaller of which acted as a feeding place and the larger (12 ins. x 12 ins. x 9 ins. high) of which held the nest. The nesting compartment was filled with moss, in the centre of which was placed a hollow sphere of cellulose wadding, about the size of a tennis ball, with a lump of fresh pollen in its cavity. As soon as a queen had laid her eggs in this cavity and had constructed a honeypot the nest-box was placed out-of-doors and the queen as allowed to fly and seek food whenever she wanted. In 1951 Hasselrot set up 30 nest-boxes in this way and in 26 of them queens started their nests. He has obtained equally good or even better results in recent trials.

What is it that appears to make Hasselrot's method superior even to that of Frison? Two differences between their respective techniques might provide the answer. Frison gave his queens plenty of exercise and let them become 'broody' before he put them into nest-boxes whereas Hasselrot kept his queens inactive in a refrigerator, and, secondly, Hasselrot provided his queens with nest-material to manipulate but Frison did not. For anybody wishing to observe the stages of colony-formation, however, Frison's method is undoubtedly the more suitable, since all one needs to do is to replace the muslin-lined roof of the nest by a sheet of glass.

It will be noted that both Frison and Hasselrot, particularly the latter, thoroughly insulated their nest-boxes, so that perhaps one of the secrets of their success may have been the maintenance of a suitably high temperature inside them. We have seen (Chapter 7, p. 57) that the degree to which the ovaries of worker bumblebees develop depends to some extent on the temperature at which they are kept, and this may also be true of queens.

Although the success obtained by other workers in this field is not comparable with that obtained by Frison and Hasselrot, it is worth considering some of the more interesting results which they obtained. Sladen was unsuccessful in his attempts to induce queens kept in solitary confinement to start nests, but was successful when he confined one or two workers with each queen, or two queens together. In the latter cases one of the queens invariably killed the other at about the time the first eggs were laid; but more recent work by other investigators has shown that this does not always happen. Sladen even found that confining a queen together with workers of a different species to herself induced her to lay eggs, although the workers gave her no assistance. It looks therefore, as though some psychological factor may be involved, and some of Free's work tends to confirm this. During experiments in 1952 and 1953 eggs were laid in 32 per cent of the cases in which queens were kept in solitary confinement, in 39 per cent when they were confined in pairs, but in as many as 87 per cent when one or two workers were confined with each queen. Not only does the presence of other bees probably stimulate a queen to lay eggs, but the period between the date of confinement and egg-laying is also shortened. (It should be mentioned here that Free now lines the floor of his nest-boxes with brown corrugated cardboard, hence the reason for its appearance in several Plates).

An almost certain way of getting a colony started is to confine several queens together in one nest-box. Although fighting invariably breaks out between them as soon as they are placed together, and a number of them may be killed, after a time they come to tolerate each others' presence, one of the queens often appearing to rule the roost. But it is a very precarious peace, and any disturbance of the nest results in renewed outbreaks of fighting. However, two or more queens will sometimes continue to help each other after the first workers have emerged, even though the queens concerned belong to different species (Pl. 24b, p. 163). If, instead of confining queens together, several workers are confined with a queen, eggs are invariably laid, but, in some cases they are laid by workers whose ovaries have developed and, as these eggs are unfertilized, only males emerge from the brood produced. There seems to be no reason why a colony should not pass through its entire life-cycle in confinement if it is suitably fed and housed; a particular *B. terrestris* colony was once kept under such conditions until 65 workers and 64 males had emerged.

In by no means every case in which eggs are laid by queens in confinement is the resultant brood successfully reared, although it is more likely to be if another queen or queens, or some workers, are present to help the queen who laid the eggs to rear her larvae. What appear to be exceptional results were obtained by Valle (1955); workers were eventually reared in 41 of the 43 colonies which had been started by queens he had kept in isolation.

A queen kept in confinement nearly always constructs her egg-cell before she makes her honeypot, just as queens do in nature, but in only about fifty per cent of cases do queens lay eggs on the pollen lumps provided for them, although when they do so their brood stands a better chance of attaining maturity. Even when the egg-cells are not constructed on pollen lumps, the presence of pollen seems essential if eggs are to be laid at all. Probably when the great majority of queens are confined their ovaries have not developed sufficiently for them to lay eggs, and a supply of fresh pollen provides the protein food necessary for ovary development to reach the requisite level.

The first piece of comb built by a queen in nature has a groove along its centre in which she lies while incubating it. Although an incubation groove may also be formed by a queen kept in confinement, it is dispensed with when more than two individuals are present together. Another feature of the combs started by several individuals together is that a number of honeypots may be built instead of the single one usually built by a solitary queen. The number built is roughly proportional to the number of bees present, presumably as a result of the increase in the amount of wax available.

For the benefit of anybody attempting to induce queens to nest in confinement it should be pointed out that it is advisable to provide each nest with a fresh lump of pollen, and to clean and refill the cup in which sugar syrup is provided, every few days. It must also be remembered that bumblebees normally keep themselves scrupulously clean and if they become wet or sticky they are very inclined to 'sulk', and will certainly make little attempt to found colonies. On this account the floor of the outer compartment of the nest-box, in which the bees will defaecate, should be covered with blotting, or corrugated, paper which can be changed periodically, and care must be taken not to spill syrup when filling the feeder.

Finally, anyone who attempts either to attract queens to domiciles, or to induce queens to lay their eggs when confined in nest-boxes, should not feel too discouraged if their results do not compare favourably with those of the workers we have mentioned. Quite rightly, work of this sort is generally only published if it has produced particularly good results; without doubt the work of numerous people who have had some, but perhaps not very much, success in their experiments has never been published.

APPENDIX III

THE IDENTIFICATION
OF BRITISH BUMBLEBEES

by Ian H. H. Yarrow

INTRODUCTION

The following key has been prepared to enable enthusiasts to name their captures with the aid of no more elaborate equipment than a good x10 pocket lens. With some experience it should be possible to achieve quite a high standard of accuracy but it must be understood that a key such as this, based largely on the colour pattern of these insects, cannot be expected to produce the results of one prepared for use with expensive binocular microscopes, for many species are more easily recognised by a glance at some microscopic structure than by their more obvious characters. As few scientific terms as possible have been used and these are explained in a brief glossary, and the complexities of geographic races or subspecies are entirely omitted although allowances have been made in order to take them through the key to their respective species. Variation, not necessarily of a geographic nature, is much more pronounced in some species than in others and, as is inevitable in an artificial key, a species name may of necessity occur in several quite different sections since the key is devised to show differences, not relationships. No "common English names" have been used because none of those proposed in the past can be in "common" use in a group of insects so unfamiliar to the amateur entomologist; instead, the Latin names devised by the original describers and listed in the "Check list of the British Hymenoptera Aculeata"*have been

*The Generic Names of British Insects—Part 5, Generic Names of the British Hymenoptera Aculeata with a check list of British species. Royal Entomological Society of London, 1937.

used even though it is now known that some of these are synonyms of earlier names and, therefore, require adjustment. This book is, however, not the place to delve into the morass of nomenclature and the subject is best forgotten, at any rate for the time being.

The present key cannot be used for the identification of bees from anywhere but the British Isles and a good example of why this is so is shown by the female *terrestris* which here is dark yellow-banded with brown tail, over most of the Continent bright yellow-banded with white tail, in Corsica black with red tail and in the Canary Is. black with white tail; some horrible mis-identifications would be the only result!

A final word might be added for those who wish to pass on to the binocular microscope technique and to the interest which attaches to relationship. The most up-to-date comprehensive work on our British species was published in 1927 by Richards (Trans. ent. Soc. Lond.) and is far and away superior to any of its predecessors but it was not intended for the novice and the keys would almost certainly be quite beyond him; it includes illustrations of the male genitalia of almost all species but no coloured plates and those wishing for such should consult F. W. L. Sladen's "The Humble-bee" (1912), which achieves a standard of reproduction quite amazing considering its date.

EXPLANATION OF TERMS USED

Abdomen The body behind the thorax and separated from it by a "waist". (Note: The true first segment of the abdomen is in front of the "waist" fused with the thorax; for convenience sake, however, the segments of the abdomen are customarily numbered from behind the "waist".)

Aberration (ab.) A variant (most easily noticed in change of colour pattern) which occurs sporadically among otherwise normal individuals.

Basitarsus The enlarged basal segment of the tarsus; sometimes called metatarsus.

Callose Lumpy, thickened.

Chagrinate Surface sculpture chagreened.

Clypeus The face below the antennae, to which the labrum (upper lip) is articulated.

Collar The anterior thoracic band of pale hairs.

Colour and colour pattern The colours referred to in the key apply to the hairs, not the underlying surface; the colour pattern is the overall effect (on us) of the varying arrangements of coloured hairs.

Corbicula The pollen-collecting apparatus on the hind tibia.

Decumbent (Of hairs), not standing erect but sloping over the underlying surface.

Disc The flat dorsal part of a tergite; the central part of the clypeus etc.

Face The front of the head, lying between ocelli and labrum (and thus including the clypeus, q.v.,); the species of *Bombus* may have the face long and narrow or short and broad.

Genital capsule The large copulatory organs of the male, dark and hard in *Bombus*, pale and softer in *Psithyrus*. Those who may eventually wish to identify their specimens on characters other than colour and with the aid of a microscope, would be well advised to pull out the capsule of all males before they dry because they provide wonderful separatory characters (which can be appreciated with a hand lens only after careful study with a microscope). Nearly all our *Bombus* and certainly all our *Psithyrus* can be safely recognised on the male genitalia alone.

Impunctate Surface sculpture not consisting of pits (punctures).

Interalar band The band of black between the wings of an otherwise pale thorax.

Malar space The "cheek", lying between base of eye and mandible; in the species with long face, the malar space may be more than $\frac{1}{2}$ the length of the eye whereas in the short faced species it is much less than this.

Melanisation The replacement, partial or complete, of coloured parts (hairs) by black.

Scutellum The hind part of the thorax, frequently pale haired.

Sternites The several visible overlapping plates (number St1-6) which form the underside of the abdomen.

Tail A rather unscientific term for the more apical tergites of the abdomen; it does not necessarily include the small last tergite (the tip of the tail) the colour of which may be different from the rest though not contributing to the overall appearance.

Tarsus The last 5 segments of the leg, the 5th carrying the claw and the first being broad and nearly as long as the other 4 together, and called the basitarsus.

Tegulae The little almost circular plates on the sides of the thorax which cover the articulation of the front wings.

Tergites The several visible overlapping plates (numbered T1-6 in female and workers, T1-7 in male) which form the upper part of abdomen.

Thorax The middle section of the body, between head and abdomen and bearing the wings and legs.

Tibia The long somewhat triangular part of the leg above the basitarsus (q.v.) (the tibia of hind-leg is used in female and worker *Bombus* for collecting pollen).

KEY TO SEX AND GENUS

1. Antenna 12 segmented, abdomen with 6 visible segments, the tip pointed and inwardly grooved to accommodate the sting . . . 2. (Females & Workers)

— Antenna 13 segmented, abdomen with 7 visible segments dorsally, 6 ventrally, the tip broadly rounded . . . 3. (Males)

2. Outer-side of hind tibia flat and bare with a well-developed corbicula; coat dense, usually completely obscuring the underlying tergites . . . *Bombus* Latreille (Species industrious, with a worker caste)

— Outer-side of hind tibia convex, covered with long hairs and without a pollen collecting corbicula; coat, especially on abdomen, thin, the tergites clearly visible through it . . . *Psithyrus* Lepeletier (parasitic and without a worker caste).

3. Hind tibia much less hairy on the outer-side than on the upper and lower "edges" thus closely approaching the corbicula of the other castes; genital capsule strongly chitinized . . . *Bombus*.

— Hind tibia very hairy all over, those on the outer-side much branched; genital capsule weakly chitinized . . .*Psithyrus*.

KEY TO *Bombus* QUEENS AND WORKERS

1. Thorax dorsally yellow, brownish yellow or reddish brown, sometimes with black mixed but the black never forming a defined interalar band . . . 2.
— Thorax differently coloured . . .6.
2. Tip of tail (T6) yellowish red . . . 3.
— Tip of tail mainly black . . . 4.
3. Abdomen yellowish brown and like the thorax frequently with much black intermixed . . . *agrorum* Fab. (Southern Britain & Ireland)
— No black intermixed on thorax, very little on abdomen and this restricted to the extreme sides of the tergites. . . *agrorum* Fab. (Scotland & Northern Britain, overlapping and inter-breeding with southern form).
4. Lower sides of thorax, underside and legs largely black . . . *smithianus* White. (Shetland, Outer and some Inner Hebrides, Arran Is. west coast of Ireland, Scilly Is., Alderney)
— These parts largely pale . . . 5.
5. No black on thorax or abdomen. Hairs at sides of T3 arise from pustules . . . *muscorum* L.
— No black on abdomen but at least a little on thorax above tegulae; hairs at sides of T3 arise from coarse, coalescing punctures; T2 normally with a very characteristic brown band . . . *humilis* Illiger.
6. Thorax brown with black interalar band; a large brown bodied species with a distinct keel on St6 . . . *distinguendus* Morawitz.
— Differently coloured species . . . 7.
7. Thorax grey or yellowish grey with black interalar band; small species with sharply pointed abdomen and very pro-nounced stripes of grey and black, the tail orange . . . *sylvarum* L.
— Thorax differently coloured . . . 8.
8. Thorax entirely black or with at most very faint traces of paler anterior and posterior bands . . . 9.
— Thorax with evident yellow collar, or scutellum or both . . . 14.
9. Corbicula and tail red . . . 10.
— Corbicula black . . . 11.
10. Apical tergites shining between the punctures; whole insect

sooty black except tail which is reddish . . . *sylvarum* ab. (a rare aberration in Britain though common in much of the Continent).

— Apical tergites dull between the punctures; base of abdomen black, sometimes with pale hairs intermixed, the dull orange-red tail and the red corbicular hairs distinguishing at once from the other black and red species *lapidarius* and *cullumanus* . . . *ruderarius* Müller.

11. Tail black or with brownish hairs intermixed, face very long; a large and usually entirely black species . . . *ruderatus* Fab.

— Tail red . . . 12.

12. Face long, tail and much of abdomen reddish, the black of T3 gradually merging into the red . . . *pomorum* Panzer (Common on the Continent but known as British from old records only).

— Face short, tail only red . . . 13.

13. Wings paler, hind basitarsi covered on the outside with yellow feathery hairs . . . *lapidarius* L.

— Wings darker, hind basitarsi with sparse unbranched hairs . . . *cullumanus* Kirby (a rare species restricted to certain of the chalk areas of the south of England).

14. Scutellum and collar yellow or brownish . . . 15.

— Not both scutellum and collar pale . . . 19.

15. Tail and most of abdomen yellowish red . . . *lapponicus* Fab. (Restricted to the *Vaccinium* areas of Devon, Wales and the north).

— Tail not red . . . 16.

16. Face short, T1 yellow, T2 black or yellow, T3 black, T4-6 white or yellowish white . . . *jonellus* Kirby.

— Face long . . . 17.

17. St6 with a pronounced keel, pale bands on thorax yellowish brown, T1, 2 & 3 often with brown apical bands; a large very short haired species . . . *subterraneus* L.

— St6 without such a keel; large and rather longer haired species . . . 18.

18. Disc of clypeus with at most small punctures, sometimes almost impunctate; yellow of thorax and base of abdomen usually bright, on the scutellum forming a crescent shaped mark; a rather rough haired species . . . *hortorum* L.

— Disc of clypeus with both large and small punctures; yellow of thorax and abdomen most often much darkened or reduced but if bright, then the scutellar mark is large, well defined and semi-circular . . . *ruderatus* Fab. (Does not occur in north or in Ireland).

19. Scutellum yellow, collar black, T1 & 2 black, tail white . . . *jonellus* Kirby.

— Scutellum black, collar yellow . . . 20.

20 Tail brown, reddish brown or yellowish red . . . 21.

— Tail white, tawny-white or yellowish-white . . . 23.

21. Most of abdomen yellowish red . . . *lapponicus* Fab.

— Tail only reddish . . . 22.

22. Very large females, the yellow of thorax and T2 with a strong brownish tinge, sometimes not very different from colour of tail, and often considerably reduced by invasion of black; yellow hairs of T2 short, of even length and erect . . . *terrestris* L. (queen not worker).

— Smaller females, the yellow of thorax and abdomen quite different from the rather gingery tail; coat much more ragged than in previous species, especially noticeable on T2 where the yellow hairs are rather long, uneven and decumbent (this band may be absent in some workers) . . . *pratorum* L.

23. Yellow bands on thorax and abdomen with a brownish tinge, tail tawny-white or white with tawny basal area . . . *terrestris* L. (workers).

— Yellow without a brownish tinge, tail pure white or pinkish white . . . 24.

24 Large or very large females, yellow band of T2 entire and composed of short, even and erect hairs . . . *lucorum* L. (Abundant everywhere and being the more northerly species completely replaces *terrestris* in the extreme north).

— Smaller species, the yellow band on T2 thin in the middle, often broken there and composed of rather longer, less even and more decumbent hairs. . . . *soroënsis* Fab.

KEY TO *Bombus* MALES

1. Thorax dorsally yellow, brownish or reddish brown, sometimes with black mixed but the black never forming an interalar band . . . 2.

— Thorax differently coloured . . . 5.

2. Lower sides of thorax, underside and legs mainly black . . . *smithianus* White.

— These parts mainly pale . . . 3.

3.Abdomen with at least some black on the tergites, often with black mixed on the thorax . . . *agrorum* Fab.

— Abdomen without black . . . 4.

4. Abdomen with distinct brown band on T2, thorax with a few black hairs above tegulae . . . *humilis* Illiger.

— Neither abdomen nor thorax with black hairs among the yellow, the former without a distinct brown band . . . *muscorum* L.

5. Thorax entirely black with no more than somewhat brownish hairs anteriorly and posteriorly . . . 6.

— Thorax, at least anteriorly yellow, yellowish brown or (especially in worn and faded examples) grey . . . 8.

6. Face long, whole abdomen and corbicular hairs black . . . *ruderatus* Fab.

— Face short, tail reddish brown . . . 7.

7. 3rd antennal segment distinctly longer than 4th . . . *ruderarius* Müller.

— 3rd antennal segment only slightly longer than 4th . . . *sylvarum* L. ab.

8. Scutellum entirely or in large part pale . . . 9.

— Scutellum black or largely black . . . 18.

9. Face very long, tail white or yellowish white . . . 10.

— Face not very long . . . 11.

10. Yellow thoracic bands broad, more sharply defined and less shaggy than in the following species; T1 yellow, T2 sometimes yellow in middle basally and with traces of a pale apical band. Long hairs on lower "edge" of hind tibia not continued round apex to meet those of upper "edge" . . . *ruderatus* Fab.

— Yellow thoracic bands not sharply defined, shaggy, especially on scutellum; T1 and base of T2 yellow; Long hairs on lower "edge" of hind tibia continued round apex . . . *hortorum* L.

11. Tail red or reddish brown . . . 12.

— Tail not red . . . 14.

12. T1 black or yellowish, remainder of abdomen yellowish red; face yellow . . . *lapponicus* Fab.

— T1 yellow or grey . . . 13.

13. T2 and remainder of abdomen red, face black . . . *pomorum* Panzer.

— T2 yellowish grey, T3 black, remainder dull red fading to orange . . . *cullumanus* Kirby.

14. Tail yellow or pinkish yellow . . . 15.

— Tail white . . . 17.

15. 3rd antennal segment not much longer than 4th and much shorter than 5th; T3 and sometimes T4 with a black band, tail pinkish yellow . . . *sylvarum* L.

— 3rd antennal segment much longer than 4th and almost as long as 5th . . . 16.

16. Abdomen entirely brownish yellow . . . *distinguendus* Morawitz.

— T6 and T7 black in the middle, pale laterally, T2 and T3 usually black or brown with pale apical bands . . . *subterraneus* L.

17. T1 and T2 and at times T3 and T4 entirely lemon yellow; larger species . . . *lucorum* L. (most).

— T1 and base of T2 only yellow; smaller species . . . *jonellus* Kirby.

18. Tail red or orange red . . . 19.

— Tail white, yellowish or pinkish . . . 20.

19. At most a faint trace of yellow on T1, T2 and T3 entirely black, remainder red . . . *lapidarius* L.

— T1 and T2 yellow (which can be much reduced or rarely absent), T3 black, T4 black or red, remainder red . . . *pratorum* L.

20. Hind basitarsis very slender towards base; 3rd antennal segment shorter than 4th; T1 and T2 yellow, T3 black, T4 reddish or white, remainder pinkish . . . *soroënsis* Fab.

— Hind basitarsi not slender towards base; 3rd antennal segment longer than 4th . . . 21.

21. Tail pure white; yellow of thorax and T2 rather paler, coat rather longer and rougher . . . *lucorum* L.

— Tail yellowish or tawny white; yellow of thorax and T2 rather browner, coat somewhat shorter and less ragged . . . *terrestris* L.

KEY TO *Psithyrus* FEMALES

1. Thorax and abdomen black, tail red, wings very dark; last
visible tergite (T6) completely dull, abundantly punctured on
disc, and with chagrinate microsculpture. Elevated process of
last visible sternite (St6) large, laterally produced and clearly
visible from above . . . *rupestris* Fab.
— Tail not red, elevated process (St6) at most just visible from
above . . . 2.
2. Thorax with anterior and posterior yellow bands . . . 3.
— Thorax with anterior band yellow. The posterier one brown
or absent . . . 4.
3. T6 shining and towards centre of disc with rather widely
separated large punctures but no trace of a median longitudinal
keel. Elevated process of St6 pointed apically. T1 and T2
black, T3, T4 and T5 at least laterally yellow, T6 with very
short upright pale hairs . . . *campestris* Panzer. (Particularly
prone to melanisation but may always be distinguished from
the other species by the type of sculpture of T6).
— T6 much less shining, the disc all over with large and small
punctures mixed and with a pronounced median longitudinal
keel; St6 with a crescent shaped elevation; T1 black, sometimes with yellow hairs mixed, T2 black, T3 black except
apical margin which may be yellow, T4 and T5 white, T6 with
short golden hairs . . . *barbutellus* Kirby.
4. St6 produced apically into a downwardly directed hook;
T1 usually with yellow hairs laterally; T2 black, T3 mainly
yellowish white, T4 white, T5 and T6 golden brown; T6
shining but with small punctures on the disc, towards apex
raised into a somewhat hollowed horseshoe shaped elevation;
tip of abdomen turned under and forwards more than in any
other species. . . *sylvestris* Lepeletier.
— St6 not produced into a hook apically, T3 with yellow
patches laterally . . . 5.
5. T6 brilliantly shining, almost impunctate on disc; yellow of
thorax and T3 pale, on the latter rapidly fading; coat somewhat shaggy . . . *bohemicus* Seidl. (a northern and western
species).
— T6 less shining, abundantly punctured over most of the disc:

yellow of thorax and T3 darker, coat very short . . . *vestalis*
Geoff. *in* Fourc.

KEY TO *Psithyrus* MALES

1. Whole insect black . . . 2.
— Some part red, yellow or white . . . 3.
2. 3rd antennal segment much shorter than 5th . . . *campestris*
Panzer ab.
— 3rd antennal segment about equal to 5th . . . *rupestris* Fab.
3. Tail red or red brown, thorax with at most indistinct pale
bands . . . 4.
— Tail yellow or white, thorax often with yellow anteriorly and
sometimes posteriorly . . . 5.
4. Tip of tail (T7) black, last visible sternite (St6) with lateral
black tufts . . . *campestris* Panzer.
— T7 red, T4-6 and sometimes T3 red, T1 and T2 usually black
but may have yellow mixed . . . *rupestris* Fab.
5. T7 red, T5 and T6 more or less black, T3 and T4 yellowish
white . . . *sylvestris* Lepeletier.
— T7 black . . . 6.
6. Whole insect black with exception of tail which is yellow . . .
campestris Panzer.
— Some part in addition to tail yellowish white . . . 7.
7. T3 with yellow patches laterally which may be extended
towards middle until they almost meet; St6 flat, not callose
towards apex; malar space shining and with at most very fine
punctures . . . 8.
— T3 black, white or yellowish white but without lateral
patches . . . 9.
8. 3rd antennal segment much shorter than 5th; T1 black or
yellow, T3 yellow but black in the middle at the base, T4 and
T5 white, T6 and T7 black, the former white laterally; coat
short, not at all ragged . . . *vestalis* Geoff. *in* Fourc.
— 3rd antennal segment as long as 5th; coloured like previous
species but yellow more extensive in fresh examples quickly
fading to white . . . *bohemicus* Seidl.
9. St6 callose towards apex, malar space strongly punctured;
T1 more or less yellow, T4 and T5 white, T6 and T7 black

the former white at the sides, coat rather ragged . . . *barbutellus* Kirby.

— St6 flat, malar space at most finely punctured . . . *campestris* Panzer. (Very liable to confusion with faded examples of *vestalis* and *bohemicus* but at once distinguished from these by the lateral tufts of black hair on St6).

THE DISTRIBUTION
OF THE BRITISH SPECIES OF
BOMBUS & PSITHYRUS

by Ian H. H. Yarrow

A. *BOMBUS*

1. *B. terrestris* (Linnaeus) Abundant throughout the British Isles becoming rare towards the north and disappearing entirely in the north of Scotland. The British form (subspecies) of *terrestris* has a buff-coloured tail in the female and is quite distinct from the white-tailed Continental and Channel Island form; female specimens which cannot with certainty be distinguished from the British are known from one to two restricted, though well separated, areas across the Channel, suggesting that our bee was at one time more widely distributed than it is now. The species has a more southerly range than the closely related *B. lucorum*, occurring commonly in southern Spain, the Canary Islands, N. Africa etc. but is apparently absent in most of Scandinavia.

2. *B. lucorum* (Linnaeus) Abundant over the whole of the British Isles; in the north of Scotland it occurs in a particularly large form with a pinkish yellow rather than pure white, tail, a form which has been treated by some German workers as a species *B. magnus* Vogt. On the Continent *lucorum* is abundant in Scandinavia but is rare in Spain, even in the north.

3. *B. lapidarius* (Linnaeus) One of our most abundant and constant species; it is widespread in Europe over the greater part of which it shows little variation; in the more southern parts, however, it produces a very strikingly coloured sub-species.

4. *B. cullumanus* (Kirby) This is perhaps our rarest bumblebee and is known only from a few chalkland localities in the south; no nest has yet been found and the captures to date are due to little more than chance. On the Continent *cullumanus* seems to be equally rare.

5. *B. pratorum* (Linnaeus) An extremely common species, until quite recently believed to be absent from Ireland but now apparently well established in several parts.

6. *B. jonellus* (Kirby) A widely distributed though local bee occurring in a number of slightly differing colour forms from Shetland to the Isles of Scilly, Ireland and southern England; some of these colour forms are treated as subspecies.

7. *B. lapponicus* (Fabricius) Restricted to the higher parts of Scotland, northern England, Wales and the south west; it is absent from Ireland. This is a very widely ranging species occurring right across northern Europe and Asia to Kamchatka and appearing in southern Scandinavia, the Alps, Pyrenees and Balkan mountains in more or less clearly defined subspecies.

8. *B. soroënsis* (Fabricius) Widely distributed though local, occurring over much of the British Isles though absent from Ireland; the colour pattern is constant from Scotland to the extreme south but on the Continent it is much more variable and divides into two geographically segregated forms, one with a white tail, the other with a red tail, this latter form not occurring in Great Britain.

9. *B. ruderatus* (Fabricius) Absent in north Scotland and Ireland but otherwise widely distributed. An entirely black variety occurs freely (var. *harrisellus* Kirby) but has no geographical significance except that it seems unknown outside the British Isles. Quite apart from the black variety, our *ruderatus* is a very sombre coloured bee and only very rarely has the yellow bands even approaching the intensity of the Continental form.

10. *B. hortorum* (Linnaeus) A common species with a more northerly distribution than *ruderatus* from which it has only of fairly recent years been certainly distinguished. In Norway *hortorum* produces an almost entirely black variety.

11. *B. subterraneus* (Linnaeus) This species must be classed as one of our less common bumblebees; it is widely distributed within

the southern half of England but is not known from either Scotland or Ireland. It is most likely to be found in collections confused with *ruderatus*.

12. *B. distinguendus* (Morawitz) Unlike most of our native species this bee is far more abundant in the north than in the south where it is indeed extemely rare.

13. *B. ruderarius* (Müller) Normally an abundant species from north to south, including Ireland; in certain parts of its European range (i.e. Brittany, north coast of Spain) a very beautiful colour form occurs in which the female has the pattern of the more northern males.

14. *B. sylvarum* (Linnaeus) Although abundant over most of England and south Scotland this species is extremely rare in Ireland. In certain parts of the Continent a very dark variety (var. *nigrescens* Perez) occurs freely with the typical form; this variety has been captured once or twice in southern England.

15. *B. agrorum* (Fabricius) A very common species almost everywhere, occurring in the north and south in two different forms which overlap and interbreed in north England and north Wales. On the Continent *agrorum* is an extremely variable bee, changing from the very dark forms of Scandinavia to the almost entirely bright fox-red forms of Spain, south of France and Italy through a number of intermediate colour forms.

16. *B. humilis* (Illiger) Far less common than *agrorum* but usually plentiful where it occurs; apparently absent in Scotland and Ireland. Whereas in England the colour pattern of this bee is extremely constant, on the Continent it is quite the reverse, varying almost as much as in *agrorum* and with roughly the same range of variation, but these colour forms show little or no geographic segregation and a great number of them may be taken with a single sweep of the net.

17. *B. muscorum* (Linnaeus) This is a species whose real distribution within our island has been much obscured by confusion with *humilis* and quite as much if not more by nomenclatorial troubles. It is decidely uncommon in the south and south east but is more plentiful in the south west, Wales, Ireland and in the north where it reaches the Orkney though not the Shetland Islands. The northern and southern forms are somewhat different and they no doubt intergrade where they meet. On

the Continent the species is widespread and compared with *agrorum* and *humilis* shows relatively little variation.

18. *B. smithianus* (White) The distribution of this bee is quite the most remarkable of all our British species. No entirely satisfactory explanation has yet been propounded and in the present limited space no reappraisal of the problem can be attempted. The facts are briefly that *smithianus* occurs in a number of rather well defined colour forms in several of the islands fringing the west and south coasts (Shetland, some Outer and some Inner Hebrides, some islands off the west coast of Ireland, some of the Scilly and Channel Islands; on the Continent it is known from some islands off the coast of Norway, in southern Finland and in western Russia). In none of the islands is *muscorum* known to occur and until very recently it was believed that *smithianus* never occurred on the mainland. Now, however, it is certain that these two occur together in southern Norway and probably also in north-west Scotland and in both these places intermediate forms also occur. It seems likely that in the future *smithianus* must be removed from its pedestal and treated as a subspecies of *muscorum* and the several forms now treated as subspecies accorded some lower significance. But whatever may be the true explanation of the "fringing" distribution of *smithianus* it is evident that *muscorum* is not suited to life on small windswept islands or it would surely have swamped (genetically) *smithianus* in these strongholds in the same way that it may possibly have done on the mainland a very long time ago.

19. *B. pomorum* (Panzer) This species is very doubtfully British and since the original captures about one hundred years ago near Deal in Kent no further evidence of its existence has come to light. Across the Channel *pomorum* is not uncommon and it is not entirely impossible for individuals to be blown across and survive our climate for a while.

B. *PSITHYRUS*

Since the distribution of a parasite can only, under the most exceptional (and disastrous) circumstances, exceed that of its host, it stands to reason that a mere host-parasite list will show the possible range of the parasite; in fact, however, this can be rather misleading, because although the presence of the parasite in some areas implies the presence of the host, the reverse is not always correct.

P. rupestris (Fabricius) Parasitic on *lapidarius* whose distribution it follows very closely.

P. vestalis (Geoffrey *in* Fourcroy) and *P. bohemicus* (Seidl). These closely related species are parastic on *B. terrestris* and *lucorum* respectively, the former, as one might expect, having a more southern distribution than the latter which is very rare in the south east despite the abundance of its host. In Ireland both *vestalis* and its host are very rare while *P. bohemicus* and *B. lucorum* are abundant.

P. barbutellus (Kirby) Parasitic on *B. hortorum* whose distribution it follows very closely.

P. campestris (Panzer) Parasitic on *B. agrorum* over the whole of the British Isles. It is probable that this species also attacks *B. humilis*.

P. sylvestris (Lepeletier) Except in Ireland this species is quite certainly parasitic on *B. pratorum* and is fairly abundant. In Ireland where, until recently *B. pratorum* was unknown, the parasitic bee is not uncommon and some alternative host must be available. The obvious choice is *B. jonellus* as this is the only Irish species closely related to *pratorum,* but I do not know of any evidence of such a relationship in England.

It will be seen from the above that at most, eight of our *Bombus* species are subject to *Psithyrus* attack but on the Continent several of our unaffected species are not so fortunate.

BIBLIOGRAPHY

General Works

MICHENER, C. D. & MICHENER, M. H. (1951). American social insects. New York: Van Nostrand.

PLATH, O. E. (1934). Bumblebees and their ways. New York: MacMillan.

RICHARDS, O. W. (1953). The social insects. London: Macdonald.

SLADEN, F. W. L. (1912). The Humble-bee, its life history and how to domesticate it. London, MacMillan.

Special References

AKERBERG, E. & LESINS, S. K. (1949). Insects pollinating alfalfa in Central Sweden. Kungl. Lantbrukshögsk. Ann. *16:* 630-43.

BAILEY, L. (1954). The filtration of particles by the proventriculi of various Aculeate Hymenoptera. Proc. Roy. Ent. Soc. Lond. *29:* 119-23.

BENNETT, A. W. (1883). On the constancy of insects in their visits to flowers. J. Linn. Soc. (Zool.) *17:* 175-85.

BETTS, A. D. (1920a). Nosema in humble bees. Bee World *1:* 171.

BETTS, A. D. (1920b). Constancy of the pollen-collecting bee. Bee World *2:* 10-11.

BLACKITH, R. E. (1957). Social facilitation at the nest entrance of some Hymenoptera. Physiol. comp. *4:* 388-402.

BOHART, G. E. (1956). Alfalfa pollination by wild bees. Int. Congr. Ent. *10.*

BOHART, G. E. & KNOWLTON, G. F. (1952). Yearly population fluctuation of *Bombus morrisoni* at Fredonia, Arizona. J. econ. Ent. *45:* 890.

BOLS, J. H. (1937). Observations on *Bombus* and *Psithyrus*, especially on their hibernation. Proc. Roy. Ent. Soc. Lond. *12:* 47-50.

BRAUN, E., MACVICAR, R. M., GIBSON, D. R. & PANKIW, P. (1956). Pollination studies on Red Clover. Int. Congr. Ent. *10.*

BRIAN, A. D. (1951a). Brood development in *Bombus agrorum* (Hym., Bombidae). Ent. mon. Mag. *87:* 207-12.

BRIAN, A. D. (1951b). The pollen collected by bumble-bees. J. Anim. Ecol. *20:* 191-94.

BRIAN, A. D (1952). Division of labour and foraging in *Bombus agrorum* Fabricius. J. Anim. Ecol. *21:* 223-40.

BRIAN, A. D. (1954). The foraging of bumble bees. Bee World *35:* 61-67, 81-91.

BRIAN, A. D. (1957). Differences in the flowers visited by four species of bumblebees and their causes. J. Anim. Ecol. *26:* 69-96.

BROWN, A. G. (1951). Factors affecting fruit production in plums. Fruit Yearb. 1950: 12-18.

BRITTAIN, W. H. & Newton, D. E. (1933). A study in the relative constancy of hive bees and wild bees in pollen gathering. Canad. J. Res. *9:* 334-49.

BUTLER, C. G. (1954). The world of the honeybee. London, Collins.

BUTLER, C. G., FREE, J. B., & SIMPSON J. (1956). Some problems of red clover pollination. Ann. appl. Biol. *44:* 664-69.

BUTTEL-REEPEN, H. VON (1903). Die stammesgeschichtliche Entstehung des Bienenstaates, sowie Beiträge zur Lebensweise der solitären und sozialen Bienen (Hummeln, Meliponinen etc.) Zool. Kongr., Giessen.

CARRICK, R. (1936). Experiments to test the efficiency of protective adaptations in insects. Trans Roy. Ent. Soc. Lond. *85:*131-39.

CHRISTY, R. M. (1883). On the methodic habits of insects when visting flowers. J. Linn. Soc. (Zool.) *17:* 186-94.

CLEMENTS, F. E. & LONG, F. L. (1923). Experimental pollination. An outline of the ecology of flowers and insects. Washington, Carnegie.

COVILLE F. V. (1890). Notes on bumblebees. Proc. Ent. Soc. Wash *1:* 197-203.

CUMBER, R. A. (1949a). Biology of humble-bees with special reference to the production of the worker caste. Trans. Roy. Ent. Soc. Lond. *100:* 1-45.

CUMBER, R. A. (1949b). Humble-bee parasites and commensals found within a thirty mile radius of London. Proc. Roy. Ent. Soc. Lond. *24:* 119-27.

CUMBER, R. A. (1953). Some aspects of the biology and ecology of humble-bees bearing upon the yields of red-clover seed in New Zealand. N.Z. J. Sci. Tech. B. *34:* 227-40.

CUMBER, R. A. (1954). The life-cycle of humble-bees in New Zealand. N.Z. J. Sci. Tech. B. *36:* 95-107.

DARWIN, C. (1841). Humble-Bees. Gdnrs.' Chron. p. 550.

DARWIN, C. (1859). On the origin of species by means of natural selection. London, Murray.

DARWIN, C. (1876). The effects of cross and self fertilisation in the vegetable kingdom. London, Murray.

DIAS, D. (1958). Sôbre a fundaçâo e ciclo das colonias de *Bombus* no Brasil. Rev. Brasil Entomol, *8:* 1-20

FANTHAM, H. B. & PORTER, A. (1914). The morphology, biology and economic importance of *Nosema bombi* n. sp., parasitic in various humble-bees (*Bombus* spp.) Ann. trop. Med. Parasit. *8:* 623-38.

FOREL, A. (1908). The Senses of Insects. London, Methuen.

FRANK, A. (1941). Eigenartige Flugbahnen bei Hummelmännchen. Z. vergl. Physiol. *28:* 467-84.

FREE, J. B. (1955a). Queen production in colonies of bumblebees. Proc. Roy. Ent. Soc. Lond. *30:* 19-25.

FREE, J. B. (1955b). The division of labour within bumblebee colonies. Insectes Soc. *2:* 195-212.

FREE, J. B. (1955c). The behaviour of egg-laying workers of bumblebee colonies. Brit. J. Anim. Behav. *3:* 147-53.

FREE, J. B. (1955d). The collection of food by bumblebees. Insectes Soc. *2:* 303-11.

FREE, J. B. (1955e). The adaptability of bumblebees to a change in the location of their nest. Brit. J. Anim. Behav. *3:* 61-65.

FREE, J. B. (1957). The effect of social facilitation on the ovary development of bumblebee workers. Proc. Roy. Ent. Soc. *32:* 182-84.

FREE, J. B. (1958a). The production of egg laying workers in bumblebee colonies. Insectes Soc. (In Press).

FREE, J. B. (1958b). The defence of bumblebee colonies. Behaviour *12:* 233-42.

FRISCH, K. V. (1952). Hummeln als unfreiwillige Transportflieger. Natur. u. Volk. *82:* 171-74.

FRISON, T. H. (1917). Notes on Bombidae, and on the life history of *Bombus auricomus* Robt. Ann. Ent. Soc. Amer. *10:* 277-86.

FRISON, T. H. (1918). Additional notes on the life history of *Bombus aricomus* Robt. Ann. Ent. Soc. Amer. *11:* 43-48.

FRISON, T. H. (1921). *Antherophagus ochraceus* Mels. in the nests of bumblebees. Amer. Nat. *55:* 188-92.

FRISON, T. H. (1926a). Contribution to the knowledge of the inter-relations of the bumblebees of Illinois with their animate environment. Ann. Ent. Soc. Amer. *19:* 203-34.

FRISON, T. H. (1926b). Experiments in attracting queen bumblebees to artificial domiciles. J. econ. Ent. *19:* 149-55.

FRISON, T. H. (1927a). The fertilisation and hibernation of queen bumblebees under controlled conditions (Bremidae Hym.) J. econ. Ent. *20:* 522-26.

FRISON, T. H. (1927b). Experiments in rearing colonies of bumblebees (Bremidae) in artificial nests. Biol. Bull. Wood's Hole *52:* 51-67.

FRISON, T. H. (1928). A contribution to the knowledge of the life history of *Bremus bimaculatus* (Cresson) (Hym.). Ent. Amer. (N.S.) *8:* 158-223.

FRISON, T. H. (1930). Observations on the behaviour of bumblebees (Bremus). The orientation flight. Canad. Ent. *62:* 49-54.

FYE, R. E. & MEDLER, J. T. (1954a). Spring emergence and floral hosts of Wisconsin bumblebees. Trans. Wis. Acad. Sci. Arts. Lett. *43:* 75-82.

FYE, R. E. & MEDLER, J. T. (1954b). Field domiciles for bumblebees. J. econ. Ent. *47:* 672-76.

HAAS. A. (1946). Neue Beobachtungen zum Problem der Flugbahnen bei Hummelmännchen. Z. Naturf. *1:* 596-600.

HAAS, A. (1949a). Arttypische Flugbahnen von Hummelmännchen. Z. vergl. Physiol. *31:* 281-307.

HAAS, A. (1949b). Gesetzmässiges Flugverhalten der Männchen von *Psithyrus silvestris* Lep. und einiger solitärer Apiden. Z. vergl. Physiol. *31:* 671-83.

HAAS, A. (1952). Die Mandibeldrüse als Duftorgan bei einigen Hymenopteren. Naturwissenchaften *39:* 484.

HASSELROT, T. B. (1952). A new method for starting bumblebee colonies, Agron. J. *44:* 218-19.

HAWKINS, R. P. (1956). A preliminary survey of red clover seed production. Ann. appl. Biol. *44:* 657-64.

HAVILAND, G. D. (1887). Humble Bees. Brit. Bee J. *15:* 217.

HIMMER, A. (1933). Die Nestwärme bei *Bombus agrorum* (Fabr.) Biol. Zbl. *53:* 270-76.

HOFFER, E. (1882). Die Hummelbauten. Kosmos, Stuttgart. *12:* 412-21.

HOFFER, E. (1882-3). Die Hummeln Steiermarks' Lebensgeschichte und Beschreibung derselben II. Halfte. 32nd Jahresbericht der Steiermarkischen Landes-Oberrealschule in Graz, 1-98.

HOFFER, E. (1886). Wunderbares Erinnerungsvermögen der Hummeln. Kosmos, Stuttgart. *18:* 111-15.

HOFFER, E. (1889). Die Schmarotzerhummeln Steiermarks, Lebensgeschichte und Beschreibung derselben. Mitt. naturw. Ver. Steierm. *25:* 82-158.

HUBER, P. (1802). Observations on several species of the genus Apis, known by the name of humble-bees, and called Bombinatrices by Linnaeus. Trans. Linn. Soc. Lond. Zool. *6:* 214-98.

HUDSON, W. H. (1892). A Naturalist in La Plata. London: Chapman & Hall.

HUISH, R. (1817). Bees: Their Natural History and General Management. London: Bohn.

HULKKONEN, O. (1928). Zur biologie der südfinnischen Hummeln. Ann. Univ. Åbo. (Turku) Ser. A 3. 1-81.

HULKKONEN, O. (1929). Die Hummeln als Gäste der Blattläuse. Ann. Soc. Zool. Bot. Fenn. Vanamo. *8:* 51-54.

IHERING, R. VON. (1903). Zur Frage nach dem Ursprung der Staatenbildung bei den sozialen Hymenopteren. Zool. Anz. *27:* 113-18.

IMMS, A. D. (1947). Insect Natural History. London: Collins.

JORDAN, R. (1936). Beobachtungen der Arbeitsteilung im Hummelstaate (*B. muscorum*) Arch. Bienenk. *17:* 81-91.

KNUTH, P. (1906-1909). Handbook of flower pollination (Trans. by J. R. Ainsworth-Davis)—3 vol. Oxford: Clarendon.

KRÜGER, E. (1951). Über die Bahnflüge der Männchen der Gattungen *Bombus* und *Psithyrus*. Z. Tierpsychol. *8:* 61-75.

KULLENBERG, B. (1956). Field experiments with chemical sexual attractants on Aculeate Hymenoptera males I. Zool. Bidr. Uppsala, *31:* 253-354.

KUGLER, H. (1943). Hummeln als Blütenbesucher. Ergebn. Biol. *19:* 143-323.

KUROTSHKIN, A. A. (1930). Experiments on an exact estimation of the work of the bumblebee on the pollination of red clover. Rep. Bur. appl. Ent. (Leningrad) *4:* 471-82.

LAIDLAW, W. B. R. (1930). Notes on some humble-bees and wasps in Scotland. Scot. Nat. *184:* 121-25, 135-36.

LEPELETIER, DE ST. FARGEAU (1836). Histore Naturelle des Insectes Hyménoptères. *1:* 435-75.

LEPPIK, E. E. (1953). The ability of insects to distinguish number. Amer. Nat. *87:* 228-36.

LEUCKART, R. (1885a). Über die Entwicklung der *Sphaerularia bombi*. Zool. Anz. *8:* 273-77.

LEUCKART, R. (1885b). Über *Sphaerularia bombi* (Nachtrag und Berichtigung). Zool. Anz. *8:* 358.

LEX, T. (1954). Duftmale an Blüten. Z. vergl. Physiol. *36:* 212-34.

LINDHARD, E. (1911). Om Rødkløverens Bestøvning og de Humlebiarter, som herved er virksomme. Tidsskr. Landbr. Planteavl. *18:* 719-37.

LINDHARD, E. (1912). Humlebien som Husdyr. Spredte Traek af nogle danske Humlebiarters Biologi. Tidsskr. Landbr. Planteavl. *19:* 335-52.

LINDHARD, E. (1921). Der Rotklee, *Trifolium pratense* L., bei natürlicher und künstlicher Zuchtwahl. Z. Pflanzenz. *8:* 95-120.

LØKEN, A. (1949). Bumble bees in relation to *Aconitum septentrionale* in central Norway (Oeyer). Nytt. Mag. Naturv. *87:* 1-60.

LØKEN, A. (1954). Observations of bumble bee activity during the solar eclipse, June 30, 1954. Univ. Bergen Årb. naturv. R. *13:* 3-6

LONGSTAFF, T. G. (1932). An ecological reconnaisance in West Greenland. J. Anim. Ecol. *1:* 119-42.

LOVELL, J. H. (1918). The flower and the bee. New York, Scribner.

MANNING, A. (1956a). The effect of honey-guides. Behaviour *9:* 114-39.

MANNING, A. (1956b). Some aspects of the foraging behaviour of bumble-bees. Behaviour *9:* 164-201.

MEIDELL, O. (1934). Fra dagliglivet i et homlebol. Naturen: 85-95, 108-16.

MEIDELL, O. (1944). Notes on the pollination of *Melampyrum pratense* and the "honeystealing" of humble-bees and bees. Bergens. Mus. Årb. naturv. R.: *11.*

MENKE, H. F. (1951). Insect pollination of apples in Washington State. Int. beekeep. Congr. *14.*

MENKE, H. F. (1954). Insect pollination in relation to alfalfa seed production in Washington. Bull. Wash. St. agric. Exp. Sta. *555.*

MICHENER, C. D. & LABERGE, W. E. (1954). A large *Bombus* nest from Mexico. Psyche, Camb., Mass. *61:* 63-67.

MINDERHOUD, A. (1949). Het gebruik van bijen en hommels voor bestuiving in afgesloten ruimten. Meded. Inst. Vered. Tuinbgewass. *17:* 32-37.

OUDEMANS, A. C. (1902). New list of Dutch *Acari.* Second Part. With remarks on known and descriptions of a new subfamily, new genera and species. Tijdschr. Ent. *45:* 1-52.

PALM, N. B. (1948). Normal and pathological histology of the ovaries in *Bombus Latr.* (Hymenopt.) Opusc. Ent. *7:* 1-101.

PEDERSEN, A. & SØRENSEN, N. (1935). Undersøgelser over rødkløverens bestøvning og angreb af spidmussnudebiller paa rodklover. Tidsskr. Frøavl. *12:* 288-300.

PEREZ, J. (1889). Les Abeilles. Paris.

PITTIONI, B. (1937). Die Hummelfauna des Kalsbachtales in Ost-Tirol. Festschr. Prof. Dr. Strand *3:* 64-122.

PLATEAU, F. (1902). L'ablation des antennes chez les bourdons, et les appreciations d'Auguste Forel. Ann. Soc. Ent. Belg. *46:* 414-27.

PLATH, O. E. (1923a). Notes on the egg-eating habits of bumblebees. Psyche, Camb., Mass. *30:* 193-202.

PLATH, O. E. (1923b). Breeding experiments with confined *Bremus* (*Bombus*) queens. Biol. Bull. Wood's Hole. *45:* 325-41.

PLATH, O. E. (1927). *Psithyrus laboriosus,* an unwelcome guest in the hives of *Apis mellifica.* Bull. Brooklyn Ent. Soc. *22:* 121-25.

POHJAKALLIO, O. (1938). Kimalainen puna-apilan polyyttäjänä. Luonnon Ystävä. *42:* 61-67.

PUTNAM, F. W. (1864). Notes on the habits of some species of humble-bees. Proc. Essex Inst. Salem. Mass. *4:* 98-105.

RAU, P. (1924). Notes on captive colonies and homing of *Bombus pennsylvanicus* de Geer. Ann. Ent. Soc. Amer. *17:* 368-81.

REAUMUR, M. de (1742). Histoire des Bourdons. Vélus, dont les Nids sont de Mousse. Memoires pour Servoir a l'Histoire des Insectes. Premiere Memoire *4:* 1-38.

REINIG, W. F. (1935). On the variation of *Bombus lapidarius* L. and its cuckoo, *Psithyrus rupestris* Fabr. with notes on mimetic similarity. J. Genet. *30:* 321-56.

RICHARDS, O. W. (1927a). Some notes on the humble-bees allied to *Bombus alpinus* L. Tromsø Mus. Arsh. *50:* 1-32.

RICHARDS, O. W. (1927b). Sexual selection and allied problems in the insects. Biol. Rev. *2:* 298-364.

RICHARDS, O. W. (1927c). The specific characters of the British humble-bees (Hymenoptera). Trans. Ent. Soc. Lond. *75:* 233-68.

RICHARDS, O. W. (1946). Observations on *Bombus agrorum* (Fabricius) (Hymen., Bombidae). Proc. R. Ent. Soc. Lond. *21:* 66-71.

SAUNDERS, E. (1909). Bombi and other aculeates collected in 1908 in the Berner Oberland by the Rev. A. E. Eaton, M.A. Ent. mon. Mag. *45:* 83-84.

SCHMIDT, W. J. (1939). Über das Vokommen von Wachs im Lumen der Chitinhaare von Bombus. Zool. Anz. *128:* 270-73.

SCHREMMER, F. (1955). Über anormalen Blütenbesuch und das Lernvermögen blütenbesuchender Insekten. Osterr. Bot. Z. *102:* 551-71.

SCHRÖDER, C. (1912). Handbuch der Entomologie. Jena: Fischer.

SCOTT, H. (1920). Notes on the biology of some inquilines and parasites in a nest of *Bombus derhamellus* Kirby; with a description of the larva and pupa of *Epuraea depressa* Illig. (= aestiva Auctt: Coleoptera, Nitidulidae) Trans. Ent. Soc. Lond. 99-127.

SKOVGAARD, O. S. (1945). Rødkløverens Bestøving, Humlebier og Humbleboer. Kl. danske. vidensk. Selsk. Nat — og. math. Ser 6(9):1-140.

SKOVGAARD, O. S. (1952). Humlebiers og honningbiers arbejdshastighed ved bestøvningen af rødkløver. Tidsskr. Planteavl. *55:* 449-75.

SLADEN, F. W. L. (1896). Humble Bees. Brit. Bee J. *24:* 37, 47-48.

SLADEN, F. W. L. (1900). Humblebees in winter. Brit. Bee J. *28:* 72-74.

SOPER, M. H. R. (1952). A study of the principal factors affecting the establishment and development of the field bean (*Vicia faba*). J. Agric. Sci. *42:* 335-46.

SPRENGEL, C. K. (1793). Das entdeckte Geheimnis der Natur im Bau und in der Befruchtung der Blumen. Berlin. Vieweg.

STAPEL, C. (1934). Om rødkløverens bestøvning i Czekoslovakiet. Tidsskr. Planteavl. *40:* 148-59.

STEIN, G. (1956a). Weitere Beiträge zur Biologie von *Sphaerularia bombi*. Leon Dufour 1837. Z. Parasitenk. *17:* 383-93.

STEIN, G. (1956b). Beiträge zur Biologie der Hummel (*B. terrestris* L., *B. lapidarius* L. v.a.) Zool. Jb. *84:* 439-62.

STEPHEN, W. P. (1955). Alfalfa pollination in Manitoba. J. econ. Ent. *48:* 543-48.

TANIGUCHI, S. (1955). Biological studies on the Japancse bees: II. Study on the nesting behaviour of *Bombus ardens* Smith. Sci. Rep. Hyogo Univ. Agric. *2:* 89-96.

THIES, S. A. (1953). Agents concerned with natural crossing of cotton in Oklahoma, U.S.A. Agron. J. *45:* 481-84.

THOMSON, G. M. (1922). The naturalisation of animals and plants in New Zealand. Cambridge Univ. Press.

TUCK, W. H. (1896). Inquiline and other inhabitants in nests of Aculeate Hymenoptera. Ent. mon. Mag. *7:* 153-55.

TUCK, W. H. (1897). Coleoptera etc., in the nests of Aculeate Hymenoptera. Ent. mon. Mag. *8:* 58-60.

VALLE, O. (1955). Untersuchungen zur Sicherung der Bestäubung von Rotklee. Suom. Maataloust. Seur. Julk. *83:* 205-20.

VERLAINE, L., (1934). L'instinct et l'intelligence chez les Hyménoptères, XXV. La spécialisation et la division du travail chez les bourdons. Bull. Soc. Sci. Liége *4:* 81-86.

WAGNER, W. (1907). Psycho-biologische Untersuchungen an Hummeln mit Bezugnahme auf die Frage der Gesselligkeit im Teirreiche. Zoologica Stuttgart. *19:* 1-239.

WESTGATE, J. M. & COE, H. S. (1915). Red clover seed production: pollination studies. Bull. U.S. Dept. Agric. *289*.

WHEELER, W. M. (1922). Social life among the insects. London: Constable.

WILLIAMS, R. D. (1925). Studies concerning the pollination, fertilisation and breeding of red clover. Aberystwyth, Bull. Welsh Pl. Breed. Sta. Ser. H., *4*, 1921-24: 1-58.

WILSON, G. Fox, (1929). Pollination of hardy fruits: insect visitors to fruit blossoms. Ann. appl. Biol. *16:* 602-29.

YARROW, I. H. H. (1943). Collecting bees and wasps. Amat. Ent. *7:* 55-81.

GENERAL INDEX

INDEX OF AUTHORS CITED

Also in the New Naturalist Library

THE WORLD OF THE
HONEYBEE

COLIN G. BUTLER

" An excellent guide to the mysteries of bee life, the fruit of years research. His book is intended for the general reader as well as for the bee-keeper and entomologist. Copiously illustrated with fine close-up photographs." *Yorkshire Post*

" Important as an exposition of a most suggestive theory, that of the ' queen substance '. The experiments behind this are fascinating." *Manchester Guardian*

" No-one could fail to be fascinated by Dr. Butler's account of the potent, but mysterious ' queen substance ', or by his beautiful bee portraits." *Sir Stephen Tallents—Sunday Times*

" A fascinating volume in the New Naturalist series, well illustrated and clearly written. It can be thoroughly recommended to all who are interested in the behaviour of animals in general as well as in that of bees themselves." *Economist*

" This is without doubt one of the best books of this century on bees." *British Bees Journal*

*With 2 colour photographs
and 87 black and white photographs
taken by the author*